THE CREATIVE

Communicating with Brush and
Pen in Graphic Design

*Illustrating the successful application of freehand
graphics in today's ever-changing world of design*

RICHARD EMERY

ROCKPORT
PUBLISHERS

First published in the United States of America by:
Rockport Publishers, Inc.
P.O. Box 396
Five Smith Street
Rockport, Massachusetts 01966
Telephone: (508) 546-9590
Fax: (508) 546-7141
Telex: 5106019284 ROCKORT PUB

Distributed to the book trade and art trade in the U.S. and Canada by:
North Light, an imprint of
F & W Publications
1507 Dana Avenue
Cincinnati, Ohio 45207
Telephone: (513) 531-2222

First published in Europe by:
NIPPAN
Nippon Shuppan Hanbai Deutschland GmbH
Krefelder Str. 85
D-4000 Dusseldorf 11 (Heerdt)
Telephone: (0211) 5048089
Fax: (0211) 5049326

Other Distribution by:
Rockport Publishers, Inc.
Rockport, Massachusetts 01966

ISBN 0-935603-61-1

10 9 8 7 6 5 4 3 2 1

Printed in Singapore

Contents

Introduction

The graphics industry has come a long way in clarifying its message as its primary concern. The media, both electronic and print, deliver a continuing evolution of startling effects and strategies that probe the most profound levels of communication. Just how effective are these advances, really?

As you examine the work reproduced in this book you will begin to discover the answer. And the answer is in the affirmative. Beautiful and provocative design is turning up around the world that clearly establishes new levels of communication. What this publication is primarily interested in is the effect that the human hand (freehand) has on this process. Much has been said about, and most of us have become heavily involved with computer imaging. But, as this volume shows, there is a very prominent role being played by freehand expression. It is not necessarily so, that because people can draw they will be more expressive or creative in their work, but without that experience it lessens the chance of creativity on a machine such as a computer.

In his book, THE CREATIVE STROKE, Richard Emery makes a strong point of the importance and necessity of maintaining the mind-hand-eye-spirit connection for that happy-accident or the creative revealed unconscious. He has gathered together some excellent examples of brush and pen work from a multi-faceted international group of artists, designers and calligraphers. They have used their talents to provide mood, movement and spontaneity in a way that might be untouchable by other methods.

When there are more media between the artist and the visual expression, then the less creative and expressive the work will be. This being the case, the brush is more distant from the canvas than fingerpainting and fingerpainting is more distant from the canvas than kissing it. The computer in that expression chain seems to be most distant. Is it because some of us cannot or will not allow it to be an artistic extension of our hands? Are we refusing to experience new creative expression tools? You will have to judge for yourself, as Richard Emery makes a strong showing for the freehand artist.

In the future, better technology for direct expression will inhabit (not inhibit) electronic configuring and I think the freehand artist will become highly integrated with the tool of the future. Some vehicles, like the Lute, will become part of an ancient instrument of fine art expression. Somehow the computer will come closer to the hand and heart for more direct expression. In my opinion there's something better out there, but right now, no matter how much we rationalize it, the hand is closer to the soul than the mouse.

Primo Angeli is the Principal of Primo Angeli Inc., a San Francisco-based marketing design firm.

A Brush WITH SUCCESS

Rediscovering the Message

The history of freehand graphics seems to date back to the cave walls of prehistoric times. There is no question that the artists were attempting to communicate something of significance to the people surrounding them or perhaps to the gods as they perceived them. It also seems obvious that the messages that were being considered were such that the spoken word or description could not sufficiently relate the essence or depth of their meaning. Something more subjective and expressive was needed; the free brushstroke, the moving line that carries emotion and expresses feelings in a way that touches, rather than informs.

This all seems very relevant to today's many worlds of communication. The ease with which information can be disseminated to the conscious world is an ever expanding miracle. We can find out about something with such ease and convenience that the need for comprehensive in-depth understanding seems unnecessary and irrelevant.

So there we are, saturated with information and yet feeling as though something is missing. Somehow the message seems cold and impersonal, and we do not have a true grasp of the situation. The world of present-day graphic design has the potential of falling into just such a trap. Computerized imagery has the facility for speed and accuracy never before available to the creative designer and the great seduction is believing that this by itself constitutes in-depth communication. Though it is undeniable that this facility is of great help and represents great progress in the field, it cannot reach the visceral subjective component of true communication.

The human hand with all its potential for intuitive and accidental expression provides the opportunity for a more complete involvement. Here is the human component with all its subtle variables and all its undercurrents of meaning and intention. It alone has the ability to reach beyond the mechanics and specifics to the level of real meaning.

It could be said that true communication in the field of graphic design is the sum result of all the many tools available, and one of these tools is the irrepressible human hand.

When a study is made of the applied (commercial) uses of the freehand brush and pen stroke, the strength of the message is even more obvious. The range of attitudes and nuances seems limitless and the restraints are only those of the designer involved. When discussing this with practicing designers the first word that is invariably mentioned is "spontaneity." Nothing portrays the sense of spontaneity more quickly and effectively than the brushstroke. The very nature of the application of this form connotes immediacy and leads the observer directly to the message. Iskra Johnson, in discussing the logo design for Kiki Sushi (Fig.1), states, "This was a very organic, spontaneous project; the flower image was painted on the 4th of July, and when the client saw it he said, 'Ah! A firecracker!' It expressed the livelier potential of the usually staid chrysanthemum." This application shows the combination of both spontaneity and the appropriate image for this client.

Fig. 1

In a similar fashion, Alan Gorelick described the mark he designed for Wampole Laboratories for a diagnostic system for meningitis (Fig. 2) as one "...intended to suggest the spontaneous sketch that a doctor might scrawl on a chalkboard." Once again how relevant the free stroke is to effective imagery. The use of the chalkboard idea to convey the sense of diagnostic work is combined with the suggested imagery of the brain and spine. This makes for very effective and direct communication.

Another place in which the immediacy of brushwork can enhance the message of graphic design is in the area of editorial layout. When given a multiple-paged project it is possible to connect all the various elements together by repeating a design spot or style throughout. This can achieve continuity and give intentional flow to the message. A good example of this is the 1990 annual report for ALLTEL Corporation designed by Beverly F. Schrager of Addison Corporate Annual Reports, Inc. (Fig 3.). She says, "In formulating the design for the ALLTEL Corporation 1990 annual report, our aim was to enhance the book's graphic impact, convey a sense of energy and excitement, and maintain type readability. We implemented different background colors in each section with a "brushed-on" treatment. Its purpose was to convey spontaneity, immediacy, quick response and creativity — some of the components of quality customer service at ALLTEL Corporation."

When discussing the use of the free hand in graphics another word immediately presents itself: "movement." What better way to show movement on the printed page than with the flash of a brushstroke. The eye is impelled to follow and to arrive at the desired spot within the design. Nothing can be more purposeful than this, and yet artistic integrity does not need to be compromised because of the need for utility. In fact, the artistic value can be significantly enhanced. A case in point is (Fig.4) where a strong directional stroke is used to give the feeling of emergency and the critical nature of immediate care in the hospital emergency room. Also, the overlapping repeated image increases the impact of the sense of movement. There is no question of the intent of the graphic and the sense of urgency it depicts.

Next comes the intriguing word "attitude." This represents the basic flavor or ground upon which a message exists. It is a very important consideration because it defines the environment that accompanies the specific idea. This is achieved by various uses of the brush and pen, by developing a style that projects the appropriate mood.

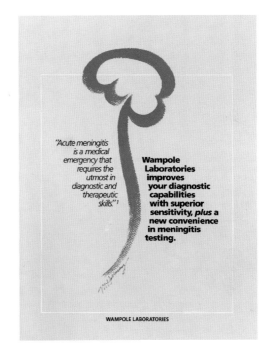

Fig. 2

Fig. 3

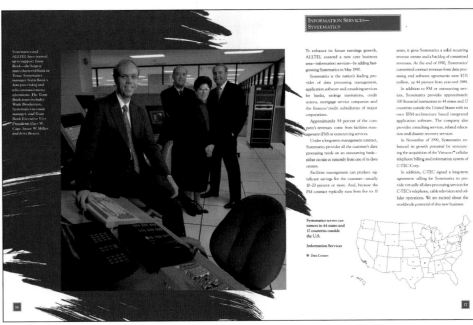

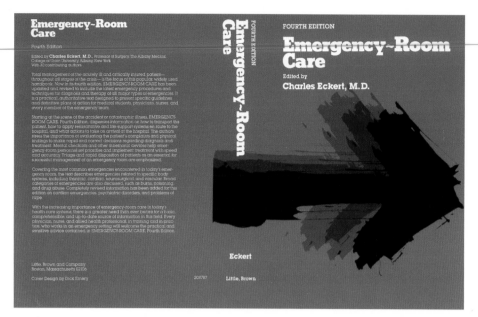

Fig. 4

Fig. 5

An excellent example of the successful implementation of the freehand stroke to achieve "attitude" is an ad designed for TRAVEL PLANNERS (Fig. 5) by Jerry Amari of Oppenheimer Advertising, Inc. Here the designer has created a pattern with a freehand felt tip line that presents the underlying quality of the intended message.

He says, "We felt that the loose line strokes, the repetition and the use of primary colors support our advertising message by giving this piece a playful, carefree quality. This effect would have been impossible to achieve through the hard pragmatism of photography or other more realistic illustration techniques." Thus this image can be carried on to other advertisements and marketing pieces to present a consistent attitude for the entire campaign.

Designer Carol Lasky along with calligrapher Jean Evans has also captured a stylistic attitude for a product logo developed for Portfolio Technologies, Inc. (Fig. 6). Prosperity, an accounting software program, is continually in the mode of reappraisal and revision and is thus never static. "In just this way, the logo (a calligraphic melding of type and mark) . . . connotes an upward growing organism. . . the unity can be seen as a composite of distinct elements." To this she adds, "The logo conveys a freedom of form that makes it decidedly contemporary. It stands in marked juxtaposition to the straight and solid grid lines that characterize the world of accounting. Its tone is positive and very much alive." The need for suggested atmosphere cannot be emphasized enough. For in truth no matter how an idea is presented it will project some form of attitude whether correct or incorrect.

In the field of graphics, the message may not always be a positive one and the attitude may need to be one of shock or horror. Take for example Figures 7 and 8. The first one was an award-winning poster against terrorism at the 1984 Warsaw Biennale designed and calligraphed by Gisela Cohrs of Germany. It incorporates a powerful use of the heavy bleeding line to project all the ugliness of the subject matter, and no one can mistake its meaning. Likewise, the calligraphy created for a book cover for Little, Brown and Co. by Richard Emery (Fig.8) depicts the explosiveness and destructive power of the atomic bomb. These pieces show the pervasive impact that the free hand can have throughout the entire field of graphic design and communication.

When venturing into the field of consumer goods and packaging there is an obvious need to establish quick identification and instant impact. Much of what is purchased either through media advertising or point-of-sale depends on the subjective impulse of the consumer, and thus the decision to purchase is made early on in the process. Therefore the more mood setting the graphics are, the quicker the response. And since we have discussed the ability of the free hand to set moods and attitudes, we are brought directly into the world of consumerism. Whether you are captured by the

Fig. 6.

Fig. 7

Fig. 8

Fig.9

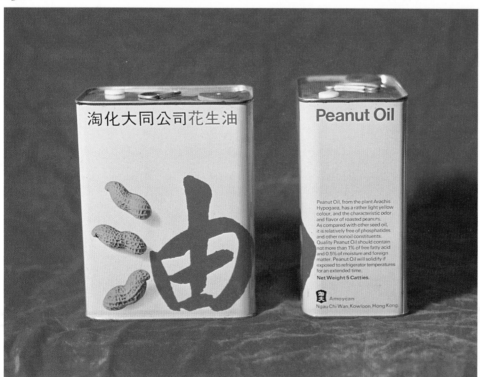

Fig. 10

delightful label for Pete's Wicked Ale, (Fig. 9) designed by Primo Angeli, or drawn directly to the bold Amoycan Peanut Oil can, (Fig. 10) designed by Henry Steiner, you cannot deny the immediate attraction they possess through the use of the brushstroke and the free hand. Much has been made of the subjective component in the advertising message and of the so-called subliminal influence. Nothing could fit more comfortably into these concepts than precisely what we are talking about here.

Finally, there is the consideration of "style." Much of what has already been said here applies to this word, and yet it can go even further. When presenting something that is truly classical in nature there can be a refinement that is neither condescending or misleading, but places the piece in its appropriate setting. Such a piece is the ad for Fine Art in Commercial Film Production (Fig. 11), art directed and calligraphed by Mary Pisarkiewicz. This is a good example of the careful consideration of the style appropriate to the piece.

When probing into the area of human spirituality and the deep meaning of faith there is a need to encompass all the joy and pain that accompanies it. Such may be seen in the simply presented "mass" (Fig.12), designed for the cover of a musical setting of the Eucharist for the Episcopal Church by Richard Emery. There is foreboding and there is hope in its boldness and directness.

Now is the time for the graphics industry to remember the rich and fertile place that the human hand has held in free artistic expression and to savor the opportunities that it still holds. May this be a continuing legacy for all the generations to come.

Fig. 12

Fig.11

If calligraphy is the art of producing beautiful or elegant writing; if it is the fine art of creating alphabetical symbols combined with beauty and legibility that please and delight the eye, then certainly Karlgeorg Hoefer is a Master of the art. His mastery is said to encompass every conceivable writing tool. He has created works with distinction everywhere he has applied his hand: calligraphy, type design, typography, book design, architectural graphics and tapestry design.

Gifted artist, influential teacher Karlgeorg Hoefer was self-taught in calligraphy, his inspiration and knowledge came from Edward Johnston and Rudolf Koch. Trained in typesetting, he completed his studies at Offenbacher Werkkunstschule before the outbreak of World War II. A prisoner af war, he returned to Offenbach as teacher and letter designer from 1946 to 1978.

It was there that he created a new pen nib, the "505" for the Brause Company. This innovative nib had a rectangular end which, when held in the proper position, produced horizontal strokes which were optically balanced with the vertical strokes. With this tool (no longer manufactured, but widely used even today by those experts fortunate enough to own one), he developed a number of typefaces; among them *Salto* his first and best known. A variety of tools including broad pen nibs, technical pens and brushes have been employed by Hoefer to develop ideas for type faces: *Prima* with the broad pen, *Zebra* with a pointed brush, *Elegance* using a Rapidograph. Yet he admits that he could not have known that the patented pen would help him with his first type design. That happened after its invention.

Koch's textbooks and writing samples were an inspiration to Hoefer during

KARLGEORG HOEFER
Discovering the Possibilities

His mastery encompasses every conceivable writing tool. He is a living master of the brush. (He) has left a body of calligraphic work, distinctive in personal style.

his typesetting apprenticeship at Offenbach encouraging his aspiration to design letters. Johnston's work gave this autodidact the opportunity to study classic examples. Free creations of all calligraphers have had the greatest impression on KGH and have moved him to try many writing tools from fibre pens and felt tips to the oriental pointed brush. He allows each tool to show him what it can do, never imitating a knowledge — of the oriental character, for example, a tradition apart from the use of the tool. Hoefer believes that just as musical instruments give sound to a composition, writing tools bring sound to calligraphy. Indeed, as his work is often described: the brush dances, the ink sings.

At Offenbach he taught calligraphy and letter design to several generations of students. After formal retirement in 1982 he founded the "Schreibwerkstatt fur jedermann" allowing him to fully develop his approach to calligraphy free from the constraints of formal courses at Offenbach. Only freehand work is created there, allowing students to enjoy the medium to the extent that their imaginations and spontaneity take them before knuckling down to technical exercises. Not only does Hoefer approach each sheet of blank paper with fearlessness, he gives his students this gift as well.

Students use only unruled paper at Schreibwerkstatt and are encouraged to see letters standing freely in space as any piece of art is, to experiment with color, light and the third dimension. Says one student, "the abundance of individual talent and sheer delight in creativity are the best reference for the work at Schreibwerkstatt. Yet probably the greatest gift was knowing that Karlgeorg Hoefer learned as much from the work of the class as it did from him. Because of that mutual respect, we all rejoiced in brush dancing and ink singing."

Experimenting with all sorts of tools one student called the work a "magnificent dance of letters, equal to that of the Baroque masters. The art of writing is alive."

Two examples of free, overlapping strokes that use varying densities and colors to bring foreground and background into play.

An example of the juxtaposition of large and small delicate strokes that have a great sense of movement and energy even though contained within one design spot.

He speaks of consistency through harmony rather than perfection.

Karlgeorg Hoefer captivates his students who span the range of age and experience, from young housewives to octogenerians, professionals and non-professionals. His joy in the everyday process of living makes it possible for him to be equally delighted with the less experienced student in the class as with the more experienced. The results of these calligraphy courses at his Schreibwerkstatt were so impressive that it was decided to present them at an exhibition in the Klingspur Museum, Offenbach. It was not long before he was in demand in workshops in the United States where he began summertime courses nationwide in 1981.

Students often speak of the invigorating atmosphere of the classroom. "He was just bursting with energy. When he entered the classroom each morning it was with a dynamic connection."

In a career that spans half a century Karlgeorg Hoefer has attained the position of preeminence among brush calligraphers in the western world. His mastery encompasses every conceivable writing tool. Yet he retains a fascination with traditional and historical forms because he feels they still have many surprises that could be developed; extracting the new from essentially old scripts. He speaks of consistency through harmony rather than perfection. It is impressive, too, that in a sometimes difficult, competitive field his colleagues know him as "a partner in fairness."

It has been said of Karlgeorg Hoefer that inspite of all his special characteristics he will let others be themselves, even though they may be contrary to his way -- a rare and laudable quality in a person and teacher.

Who is this man who brings such enthusiasm and high energy to his work? Described as having a zest for life, an infectious temperment, and thoroughness of knowledge and skill he sees his life as shaped by three concepts: the beginning, the moment, and most importantly the "it." "I always want a new beginning," he says, "and at the end of a day, I look back on a long line of individual moments. One must always continue to make new beginnings and one must act in the moment."

This attitude toward a new creation does not imply an indifference toward completions; it is more that he sees a finished form imbued with rich potential. Furthermore, he feels that if the end product becomes the focus, the means becomes a task only to be endured, and inevitably producing fear and anxiety. "There should be character, joy and pleasure," he says.

A colleague remarks, "What delights KGH is the process of creation. For him that includes physical involvement originating perhaps in his innate enthusiasm and energy and including specific exercises so that the whole body may be prepared for the motion that propels arm, hand and tool. He sees the excitement in the way the brush caresses the paper, the flow of the ink, color, even the image created by the ink on the reverse side of the page. An exercise he himself uses and recommends to his students is called Bewegung-Gegenbewegung (movement-countermovement). In this exercise, students do not make letterforms, rather they try to make spontaneous abstract writings that employ movement and countermovement, rhythms and harmony, tension and excitement, balance and proportion. One utilizes dynamic forces for basic elements which become the new vocabulary for building pictures."

Professor Albert Kapr makes the following statement: "Between calligraphy and graphics, a further interesting field of scriptoral graphics opens up, an experimental field which opens the apparent limits to the pictorial language as well as the spoken language. I call this kind of intuitive representation simply scripturen. By this I mean rhythmic writing, and drawing compositions which have been created

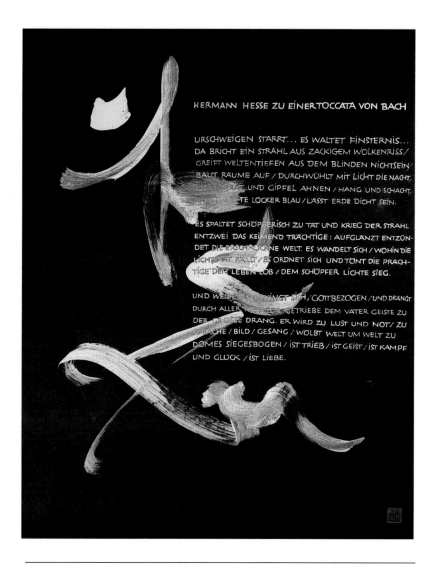

He allows each tool to show him what it can do, never imitating a knowledge.

The Chinese-like characters give an Oriental cast to the text above.

The work at left is as if a new alphabet has been born, as the broad-textured chiselstrokes speak of order, delight and fantasy.

spontaneously in moments of strong concentration. They are intuitive traces for the purpose of graphical translation of music, poetry, drama, the world of fantasy or dance."

Colleague and co-teacher, Larry Brady says "Hoefer's scripturen cannot be judged or described using the ordinary syntax of calligraphy. Rather words like movement, expression and contrast of line are the criterion for creating dynamic rhythms."

Hoefer's attitude extends beyond tools to media and language and reflects a consuming interest and openness that allow him to experience life without preconceptions which is not to say he disregards the traditional or technical parts of his work. He retains a fascination with traditional and historical forms because he feels that they still have many surprises that could be developed. "His importance internationally," says Professor A. Habley, "stems from the way new possibilities emerge in the certainty with which Hoefer recognizes, uses and at the same time overcomes tradition." Never complacent, once having developed something he is already looking ahead to what can be done next. Because he not only brings an openness and enthusiasm to the

classroom but also articulates his ideas with clarity and focus, he is an extraordinarily gifted teacher. What delights Karlgeorg Hoefer are the possibilities that emerge from a completed work; ideas gained from observation and use.

Art historians may quibble that formal scripts have degenerated under cursive influence, cursive scripts have been elevated to calligraphic status, and the history of calligraphy has been a long alternating process of loss and recovery. Karlgeorg Hoefer has shown that the emphasis on process rather than form does not neglect the calligrapher's responsibility to create legible, beautiful characters with harmony of proportion, but enhances the process by allowing it to be a means for personal expression and growth. This influential teacher and gifted artist has left a body of calligraphic work, distinctive in personal style. As he says:

Writing is not a question of tradition or restoration, of setting an example or imitating alone; it is coming to terms with the present and future. Calligraphy is not for results but for possibilities.

Patricia Pickens Emery

Hoefer's attitude extends beyond tools, to media and language and reflects a consuming interest and openness.

An abstracted monogram of swirls and leaps that give an image of constant movement and yet a sense of balance and control.

Media Advertising &
Direct Mail

The following two pieces are examples of the use of the freestroke to enhance the intended image and effect of the products involved. **Jean Evans**, the the calligrapher, has created two very different images. The first incorporates the loose brushstroke to project the sense of fine art. These graphics were a part of a service awards program for NYNEX and therefore appropriate to the quality of the objects involved. The second example shows the use of the penstroke in an abstract form to create a background for these delicate Murano Glass Quill Pens from Marcovici Designs.

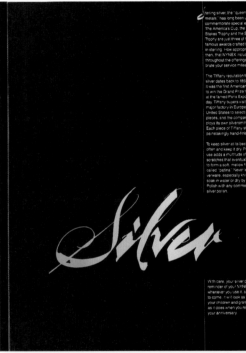

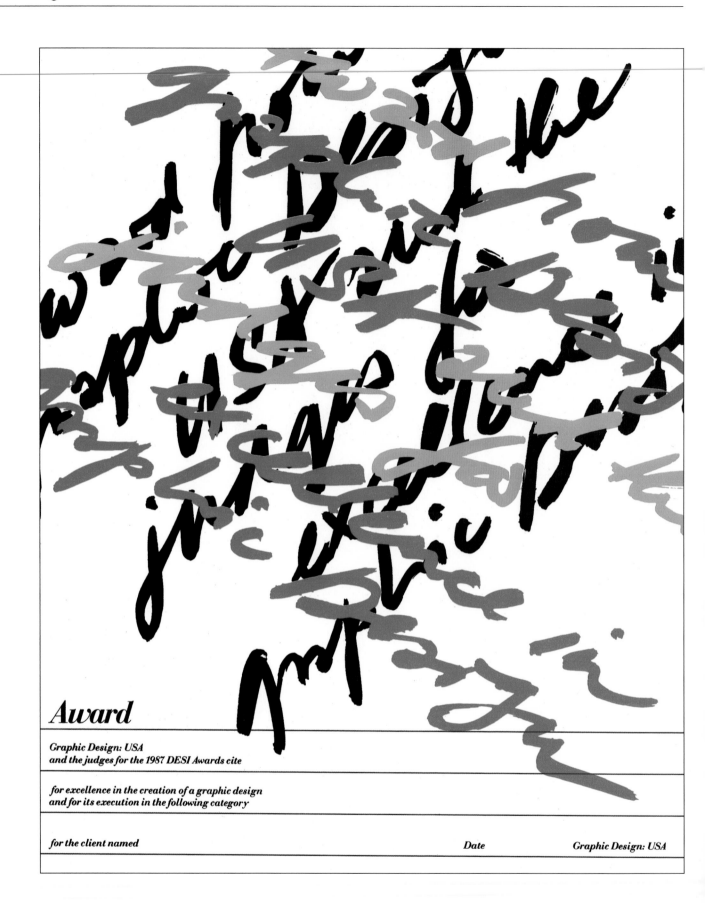

Award

Graphic Design: USA
and the judges for the 1987 DESI Awards cite

for excellence in the creation of a graphic design
and for its execution in the following category

for the client named   **Date**   **Graphic Design: USA**

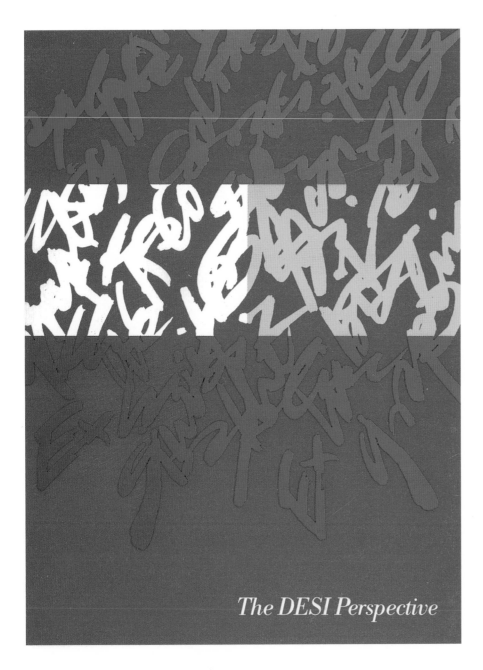

The DESI Perspective

Red Hot & Blue

Fred Troller has established a wonderful sense of superimposed graffiti for the backgrounds of both the DESI Design Award certificate *(far left)* and the exhibit invitation *(top)*. This theme was carried through with posters and ads giving the feeling of spontaneous handwriting. The third example is a dinner/dance invitation that uses the brushstroke to transform musical notes into dancing figures.

The work spread out
on page 25 displays
the unlimited scope of
the freehand approach.
Susan Skarsgard has
gathered together
these examples of her
design work to show what
can be accomplished
for a single client through
imagination and a
sense of the possibilities
of the brushstroke.
She has a unique
sense of flair and move-
ment that carries through
all of this work estab-
lishing consistency
as a prime element in the
battle to communicate.
Pictured below is an
example of how beautiful
calligraphy can provide
the perfect accompaniment
to a message, and not just
be the literal message itself.

Here are three coordinated pieces designed for Susan Bristol, Inc., using the calligraphy of **Raphael Boguslav**. This delightful use of the rough brushstroke carries with it the sense of emerging spring and the freedom that promises, while retaining the image that this is a fashion statement.

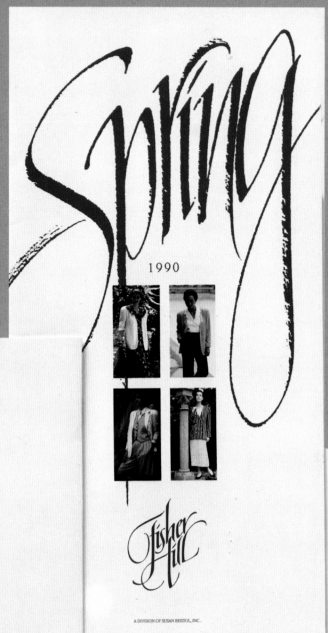

Here *(top)* Raphael has again used the rough brushstroke to project the spirit of spontaneous movement in this advertising campaign spot for Numerica Bank. The designer of the campaign was Elaine Krause of O'Neil Griffin. *Below,* a project for MetLife where he used two very different scripts — one loose and rough, one refined and elegant — to differentiate between two policies being marketed simultaneously.

GO FLY AN
O-DAKO

The fighting kites of Asia fly in the same kind of environment you deal with every business day. A competitive one.

So, in the spirit of competition, Northwest has a way to keep you ahead of the rest of the field. Our schedule.

We fly daily to Asian business centers like Tokyo, Seoul, Taipei, Osaka and Hong Kong. On nothing but 747s.

In fact we fly to more of the Far East from more of the U.S. than any other airline.

So call your travel agent, or Northwest at 1-800-447-4747. When it comes to competition, we can make you a true champion.

©1988 Northwest Airlines, Inc.

LOOK TO US NORTHWEST AIRLINES

On this spread are examples of a simple illustrative brush style that presents a bold and direct image. **Mike Quon** depicts the fighting kites of Asia *(far left)* in bold, colorful strokes. This gives the effect of the Orient that is inherent in the message of the ad. On this page are two examples of his successful use of the brush in black and white. These ads, one for Hennessy *(top)* and one for ChemLawn *(bottom)*, have a subjective nature to them that is directly attributable to the freehand style used.

On these two pages are designs by **Robert Boyajian** of new York City. *(Above)*, a single piece designed for Byron Weston with a delightful mixture of effects related to the brushstroke. Here is a combination of colors, metalic foils, embossing and freehand brush accompanying the message of "Whisper". *(Opposite)*, pieces from a calendar design showing different calligraphic treatments of the names and days of the months.

3	4	5	6	7	8	9	10	11	12	13	14	1/15	2/16
17/31	18	19	20	21	22	23	24	25	26	27	28	29	30

Develop your visual memory.

—R. HENRI

S	M	T	W	T	F	S
1	2	3	4	5	6	7
8	9	10	11	12	13	14
15	16	17	18	19	20	21
22	23	24	25	26	27	28
29	30					

For tis the mind
that makes the body rich.
—SHAKESPEARE

Here are some examples that fall into the area of pure calligraphic use of the free hand. **Larry Ottino** is creative director of The Ace Group and presents here some pieces of script art expressing flair that appears casual yet quite intentional in their form and design. These all represent headlines or titles that introduce products, people and ideas. The piece in the middle was printed on T-shirts for a promotion for the Nabisco Co. in New Jersey.

Finance Holiday Reception and Dinner Dance

December 7, 1989
GE Guest House
Fairfield, CT

_____ *We accept your kind invitation for Thursday evening, December 7, 1989*

_____ *We regret that we shall be unable to attend*

_____
Name

Barbara Harper created these wonderful pieces for a holiday dinner/reception for GE. Once the stroke was created by free-hand, it was then silk screened over solid copper and gold foil stocks allowing the metallic color to show in the negative areas.

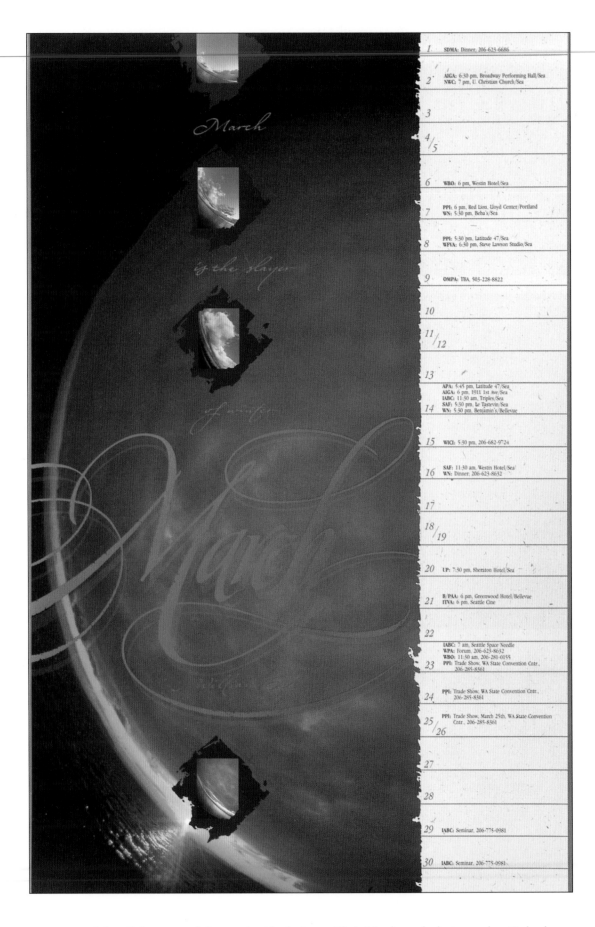

Iskra Johnson collaborated with designer Chris Maple and photographer Dale de Gabreille to create this promotional calendar for a printing firm. The freehand work is the coordinating element in this piece, establishing mood and effect quite well.

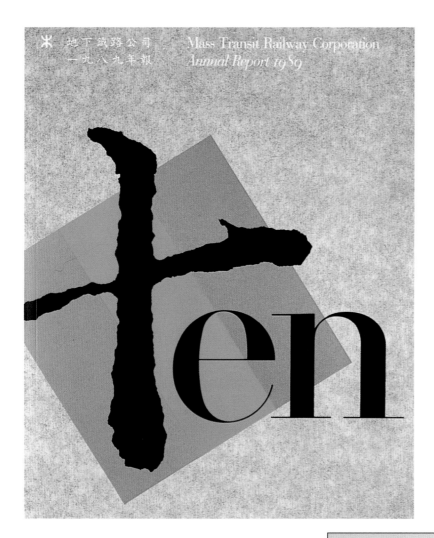

This cover for an annual report for the Mass Transit System of Hong Kong won 'Best Annual Report Award 1990' organized by The Hong Kong Management Association. **Henry Steiner** combined the ideogram for 'ten' with the roman letters to create this highly effective and representational image.

Anthony Block created this whimsical script in answer to the art director's request for a sensuous type design. It appeared as a headline in *Rolling Stone* magazine.

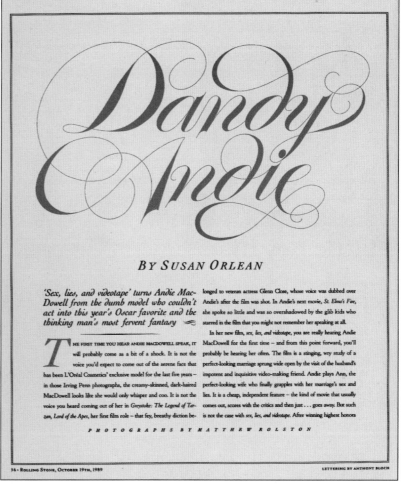

Here **Jean Evans** has created an adaptation of the classical freehand script to give the effect of combining the modern and the traditional styles. The combination of her calligraphy, the design of Corey McPherson Nash and the photography of Eric Roth creates a refined yet modern tone to this tribute piece.

TRIBUTE TO

Jordan Hall

NEW ENGLAND CONSERVATORY OF MUSIC

BOSTON

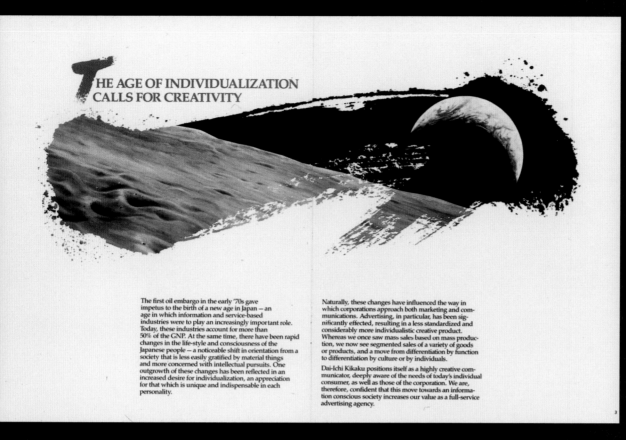

THE AGE OF INDIVIDUALIZATION CALLS FOR CREATIVITY

The first oil embargo in the early '70s gave impetus to the birth of a new age in Japan – an age in which information and service-based industries were to play an increasingly important role. Today, these industries account for more than 50% of the GNP. At the same time, there have been rapid changes in the life-style and consciousness of the Japanese people – a noticeable shift in orientation from a society that is less easily gratified by material things and more concerned with intellectual pursuits. One outgrowth of these changes has been reflected in an increased desire for individualization, an appreciation for that which is unique and indispensable in each personality.

Naturally, these changes have influenced the way in which corporations approach both marketing and communications. Advertising, in particular, has been significantly effected, resulting in a less standardized and considerably more individualistic creative product. Whereas we once saw mass-sales based on mass production, we now see segmented sales of a variety of goods or products, and a move from differentiation by function to differentiation by culture or by individuals.

Dai-Ichi Kikaku positions itself as a highly creative communicator, deeply aware of the needs of today's individual consumer, as well as those of the corporation. We are, therefore, confident that this move towards an information-conscious society increases our value as a full-service advertising agency.

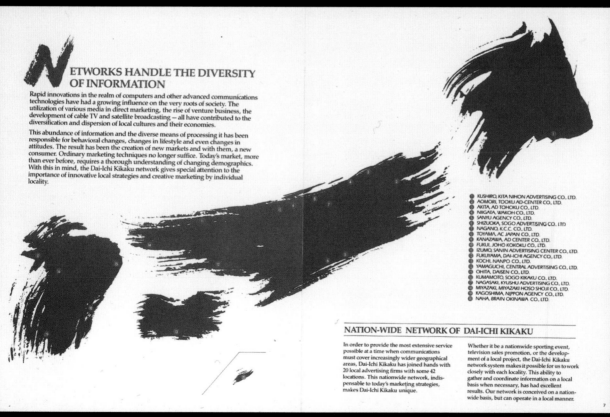

NETWORKS HANDLE THE DIVERSITY OF INFORMATION

Rapid innovations in the realm of computers and other advanced communications technologies have had a growing influence on the very roots of society. The utilization of various media in direct marketing, the rise of venture business, the development of cable TV and satellite broadcasting – all have contributed to the diversification and dispersion of local cultures and their economies.

This abundance of information and the diverse means of processing it has been responsible for behavioral changes, changes in lifestyle and even changes in attitudes. The result has been the creation of new markets and with them, a new consumer. Ordinary marketing techniques no longer suffice. Today's market, more than ever before, requires a thorough understanding of changing demographics. With this in mind, the Dai-Ichi Kikaku network gives special attention to the importance of innovative local strategies and creative marketing by individual locality.

- KUSHIRO, KITA NIHON ADVERTISING CO., LTD.
- AOMORI, TOOKU AD-CENTER CO., LTD.
- AKITA, AD TOHOKU CO., LTD.
- NIIGATA, WAKOH CO., LTD.
- SANYU AGENCY CO., LTD.
- SHIZUOKA, SOGO ADVERTISING CO., LTD.
- NAGANO, K.C.C. CO., LTD.
- TOYAMA, AC JAPAN CO., LTD.
- KANAZAWA, AD CENTER CO., LTD.
- FUKUI, JOHO KOKOKU CO., LTD.
- IZUMO, SANIN ADVERTISING CENTER CO., LTD.
- FUKUYAMA, DAI-ICHI AGENCY CO., LTD.
- KOCHI, NANPO CO., LTD.
- YAMAGUCHI, CENTRAL ADVERTISING CO., LTD.
- OHITA, DAISEN CO., LTD.
- KUMAMOTO, SOGO KIKAKU CO., LTD.
- NAGASAKI, KYUSHU ADVERTISING CO., LTD.
- MIYAZAKI, MIYAZAKI HOSO SHOJI CO., LTD.
- KAGOSHIMA, NIPPON AGENCY CO., LTD.
- NAHA, BRAIN OKINAWA CO., LTD.

NATION-WIDE NETWORK OF DAI-ICHI KIKAKU

In order to provide the most extensive service possible at a time when communications must cover increasingly wider geographical areas, Dai-Ichi Kikaku has joined hands with 20 local advertising firms with some 42 locations. This nationwide network, indispensable to today's marketing strategies, makes Dai-Ichi Kikaku unique.

Whether it be a nationwide sporting event, television sales promotion, or the development of a local project, the Dai-Ichi Kikaku network system makes it possible for us to work closely with each locality. This ability to gather and coordinate information on a local basis when necessary, has had excellent results. Our network is conceived on a nationwide basis, but can operate in a local manner.

Minoru Morita has established a bold and direct approach to the use of the brushstroke (above). By using large, free strokes as the window for the artwork and the assimilation of a map, the Dai-Ichi-Kikaku network system conveys a bold and innovative image.

On this page **Paul Shaw** has combined with Art Director David Wilder to create this delightful image for CBS Television and the Masters Tournament. One can sense the grandeur and country club setting in both the illustration and the lettering. On the opposite page *(top)* he has produced a bold yet feminine script for this salute to Esteé Lauder. For the spread from a Harmon-Kardon product catalog *(bottom)*, Paul teamed up with Janice Carapellucci to produce this striking effect. Notice the effective use of the broken-line script while maintaining its direction and flow.

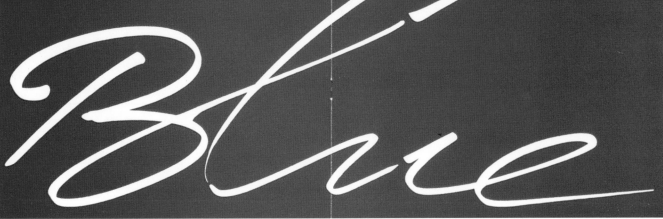

A single clarinet note squeezes out of the speakers, lazily extending itself–a long, sinuous snake of a note hanging languorously in the air, stretching up, up and finally blooming into the hauntingly familiar melody that opens George Gershwin's magnificent *Rhapsody in Blue.*

Sassy, sexy, sophisticated and sentimental, this beloved work became a permanent part of the world's musical treasury when it was first performed at New York's Aeolian Hall on February 12, 1924. The *Rhapsody* blends America's freewheeling folk music, jazz, with the more formal structures of classical music. It is a breathtaking tour de force that stirs the short hairs at the nape of one's neck and sends chills down the spine.

For the true music lover, it is the kind of listening experience that makes state-of-the-art stereo equipment one of the prerequisites of life. A fine recording of this stunning composition tests the mettle of the system employed to reproduce it. *Rhapsody in Blue* flies from delicate moments of barely perceptible solo-piano ruminations to great, crashing orchestral climaxes that have been known to shake the floors of concert halls throughout the world. It contains a host of tonal nuances and instrumental details that are essential to the character of the piece. Equipment that can accurately reproduce every precious millisecond of Gershwin's musical genius is what the passionate listener requires.

A controversial 1985 recording of the piece, with Michael Tilson Thomas both at the piano and conducting the Los Angeles Philharmonic, attempts to present the work as Gershwin originally intended. When first performed by Paul Whiteman's Orchestra with Gershwin himself at the piano, the *Rhapsody* featured orchestrations by Ferde Grofe, who rigorously followed the composer's indications for instrumentation. Grofe later rescored this concerto for jazz band and piano, for a larger concert orchestra and, after Gershwin's death, for a full symphony orchestra, the version in which the *Rhapsody* is most commonly performed today.

Thomas's restored version is a rich, thrilling blend of beauty and bombast, with extraordinary instrumental coloration that must be heard to be believed. Listen, for instance, to the introductory passage containing three clarinet notes, each almost subliminally etched with the sharp buzz of a violin. Or, later, to the lovely, fluttering piano variation on the main theme embellished with an amusing, squat bassoon–the aural equivalent of a jolly, cigar-smoking fat man rushing into a party with a willowy, flirtatious young girl on his arm.

Every instrument in this amazing arrangement is run through its paces. Trumpets are called on for clear, golden tones, then stripped of all dignity–they're muted and made clownish, forced to sway drunkenly through bar upon bar of orchestration, even reduced to the most vulgar of expressions, the raspberry. Strings buzz sharply and sing sweetly, sometimes adding a delicate filigree to a muscular piano passage, at other moments weaving a sweet, soaring cloud of violins behind a majestic orchestral movement. The percussion section makes itself known with a tinkling of chimes, the distant thunder of a soft drum roll, the heart-stopping crash of what sounds like the world's largest cymbals.

Particularly noteworthy are the silvery single chime notes that pierce the swelling orchestral vista like tiny, glittering stars in a velvety blue-black sky. Shortly thereafter,

these lovely chimes fall to earth from above, clustering to form a twinkling bridge from swelling orchestral shores back to a solo piano statement of the main theme. The piano is the driving force of *Rhapsody in Blue*, the solo instrument that sets the pace of the piece.

Under Thomas's swift, supple fingers, the piano alternately meanders onward, hesitant and drifting, then fuels a frenzied, headlong thrust that makes the music an unstoppable juggernaut headed toward its final, heart-stopping conclusion. The sense of propulsion is quite impressive, as is Thomas's astonishing flexibility, which repeatedly creates the illusion that four hands are at work here instead of two.

Thomas took great pains to be true to the spirit of Gershwin's original solo performance, calling upon the advice and remembrances of the composer's brother and collaborator, Ira Gershwin, and upon many others who were present at the premiere concert in 1924. Thomas's interpretation of the piece is an attempt to accurately re-create the thrilling music that the ingenious American composer first envisioned when his ideas were fresh and new to a world that held jazz and classical music as two separate, incompatible entities.

Harman Kardon strives to do no less. To accurately reproduce the world's great musical masterpieces is its raison d'etre. The soft drum roll that loses definition and turns to static on lesser equipment, the momentary violin hum that never reaches the eardrum–these will never be found in Harman Kardon components. The vast dynamic range of a piece like *Rhapsody in Blue* demands reproduction without distortion, and the piece's amazing palette of tonal nuance deserves to be heard in all its brilliant, colorful detail.

George would have wanted it that way.

Once again, black and white newspaper advertising becomes the perfect spot for the freehand stroke. In these two ads designer Masakazu Fujii uses the childlike gesture sketches of **Hideyuki Kawarasaki** to express a playful attitude that works well with the simple directness of the typography.

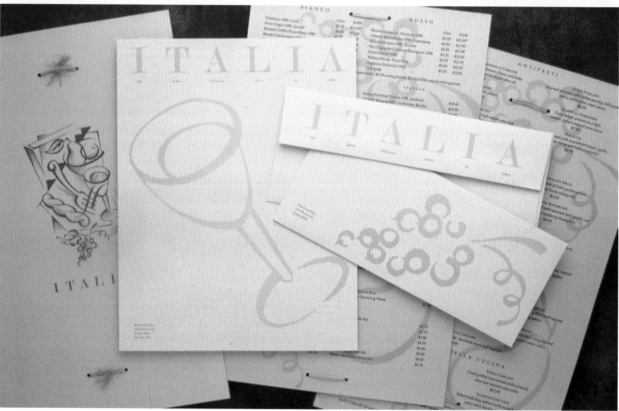

Freehand brushwork can also have its subtle application. Here are two examples of calligraphic art used in the understated association with the other elements of their design. **Jennings Ku** created the top example for HONGKONGBANK International by lightly printing the initials GAP as a background motif both on the cover and inside. The bottom example shows how **Jack Anderson** and **Julia LaPine** of Hornall Anderson Design Works used this background idea on all the collateral materials for the Italia Restaurant.

Color can have a direct impact on the successful message. *Below,* we see where bright and primary colors are used to carry the impression of a holiday spirit. **Ricardo Rousselot** of Barcelona has this spirit about his own work in this self-promotion piece *(left)* where he includes the full spectrum in his brushwork. *On the right,* **Mike Quon** captures the vacation attitude with this piece designed for AT&T. Though this design is mainly illustrative, the freedom and simplicity of its linework makes it very much a part of the basic concept of this book. While we do not wish to deal with pure illustration in this project, it seems appropriate to include work where the simplicity and directness of the art is a result of freely-expressed brush and penwork.

Frank Riccio uses his talent with the brush and pen to both illustrate and calligraph his work. *On this page,* two examples of this. *Left,* a self-promotion piece that employs a strong combination of art and calligraphy. *Right,* a highly imaginative self-promotion piece that again uses the combination of art and letter forms to tell a story while at the same time displaying his unique style and design approach.

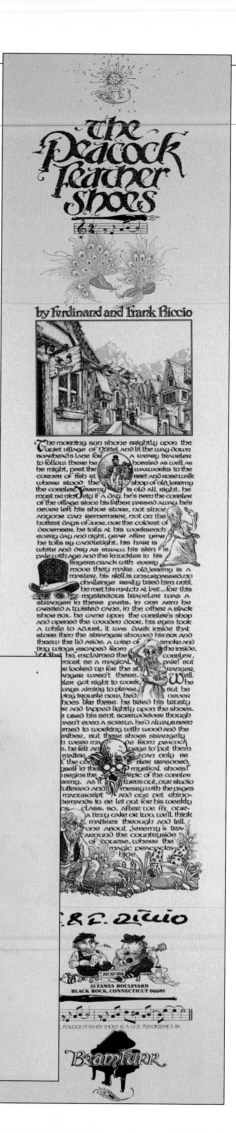

When you consider something as traditional as a wedding announcement/invitation you might not think of freehand script as an appropriate element. Here **Susan Skarsgard** uses her remarkable talent to demonstrate just how special this piece can be and how it can clearly display the feelings generated by this truly significant event.

Here again we are dealing with pure calligraphy. **Félix Beltrán** of Mexico has produced these beautiful scripts each for different purposes. *Top,* example on this page was meant to evoke a sense of "freshness" for South America Travels, Miami. For Stephanie Flowers, Miami, the feeling is of sophistication. *Opposite page, top,* a promotion piece for an office of consultants in administration with the main purpose of establishing the traditional nature of the message. *Opposite page, bottom left,* a piece done for the same group with much of the same intention. For John Hamilton Real Estate, Felix created the final piece to evoke the tradition and celebration of the holiday season.

Kevin Horvath of Overland Park, Kansas, has handcrafted these examples of script in a purposeful style that attends to the function of each piece. *Top left and top right,* two designs for Hallmark cards; *bottom,* an invitation to a V.I.P. party for Goode-Ordemann Builders-Developers.

Here we have the work of **Raphael Boguslav**. The "Cat" lettering *(above)* was suggested for a book promotion, and the imaginative numbers 1 through 5 were used as floor designations as well as in advertisements in the New York Times for B. Altman.

The three pieces on this spread are works of **Paul M. Breeden** of Sullivan, Maine, and show a diversity of style in the use of the free hand. The colorful "Web of Life" piece was created for the Lane Stewart Agency and carries with it a sense of Native American art and an interesting effect of letterform over illustration. *Opposite page top*, a delightful play with color and wash for the Raven Forge. This is a unique combination of thin line, heavy line, texture, color and prepared background. The "Celebration" spot *(bottom)* was created for One City Center, Portland, Maine, as a promotional spot that exists in contrast with the other pieces shown here.

Ron Brancato was the artist/designer assigned to these three pieces. *Top right,* a folder promoting "The Learning Environment" program for Eastman Kodak Company. The other two pieces *(top left, bottom)* were done for the Mary Cariola Creative Team for their Children's Center. The graphics show an image that is caring yet purposeful.

John Stevens created these two pieces *(top right)* for a memorial exhibition catalog honoring Guilermo Rodriguex-Benetiz in San Juan, Puerto Rico. *Below*, a seasonal image John created for United Airlines.

'Georg Trump as Artist and Man'
Vita Activa, copyright 1969

Some years ago, at a dinner given by Charles Peignot in Paris to a group of French typographers, the question arose: Who has most deeply influenced European typography in this century? A few minutes of discussion produced an admiring unanimity upon a single force: Ernst Schneidler of Stuttgart. And, it soon became clear that Schneidler's influence is being steadily extended by the continuing work of his pupils, such as Imre Reiner, Walter Brudi and Georg Trump, along with others just rising to fame. I considered this French tribute as high as any that Schneidler could have, and the ensuing years have confirmed this high rating. His most responsive pupils, such as those just named, never felt themselves constrained. Personal gifts were never made to seem antagonistic to the job in hand: they had only to be kept subordinate. What Schneidler supremely gave his pupils was a versatility in styles, proceeding from a deep respect alike for the word and for the letter. His own scribal experiments (preponderantly using texts of early English poets) gave him a devotion to the shape of words in every style of letter. Such a devotion, linked to their native talents, produced in his students a loyal and affectionate respect for language, a respect that prevents all excess in their design of letter forms.

Here we have examples of the use of the letterform as the main unifying design element in a series of spreads from a booklet for the typecrafters' *Observations of a Resolute Outsider*. **Rick Cusick** was very successful in maintaining the style and typographic consistency necessary.

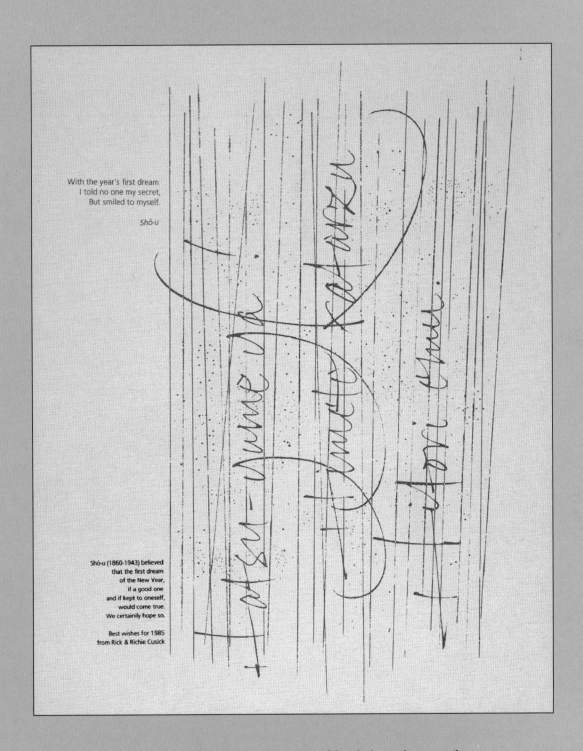

With the year's first dream
I told no one my secret,
But smiled to myself.

Shō-u

Shō-u (1860-1943) believed
that the first dream
of the New Year,
if a good one
and if kept to oneself,
would come true.
We certainly hope so.

Best wishes for 1985
from Rick & Richie Cusick

Above, Rick employs a series of fragile lines that contribute structure and a visual tension to his graceful script. This application truly enhances the spiritual content of the message which was his own personal new year's greeting.

Native influences.
Here Ralph Lauren
honors the true spirit of
the old west, beginning
with his buckskin jacket.
Soft, creamy leather
with an American Indian
handpainted on back.
The chambray work
shirt and twill jodhpur
pants finish the look in
pure cotton. Jacket,
sizes S,M,L, 1,500.00.
Shirt, sizes 4 to 14,
59.00. Jodhpur pants,
sizes 4 to 14, 90.00.
Ralph Lauren. At State
St., Old Orch., Oakbrook,
Water Tower, Lake
Forest, Mayfair, Houston
Galleria, Dallas Galleria
and Columbus.

From nouveau navajo to safari chic,
spring 1990 wears the ethnic charm
of its native influences (very) well, indeed.

Here **Eliza Schulte** of Woodstock,
Illinois, has achieved with her
letterforms a rustic primitive feeling in
this promotion for Ralph Lauren
fashion. The rough brushstroke
suggests the native culture that
influenced his design. This piece was
done with creative director Thomas
Smallwood for Marshall Field's.

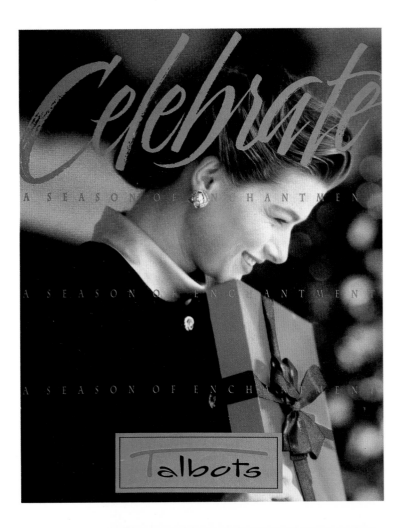

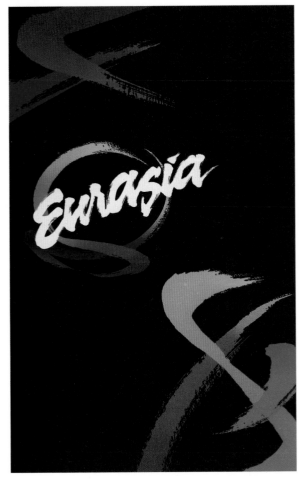

(Top left), together with art director Richard Johnson, Eliza has given a sense of celebration to this promotion piece for Talbots. With Jim DeYoung she has adapted the classic fashion script *(top right)* for the Spiegel catalog. *(Below),* a colorful and bold invitation to Eurasia created for art director Dave Pierce of the Tassani Agency.

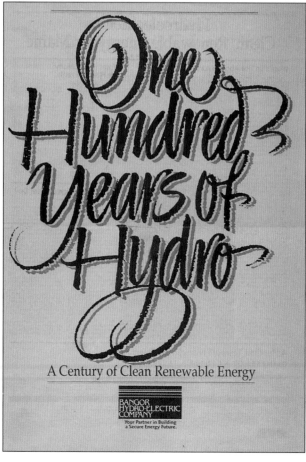

These menu covers *(top)* designed by Ken Krause of Creative Design & Marketing utilize a casual script by **Bonnie Spiegel** of Portland, Maine, to give the image of vacation time for the cruise ship *Scotia Prince. (Below),* her lettering is used on a newspaper insert for art director Bruce Hansen for the Bangor Hydro-Electric Company.

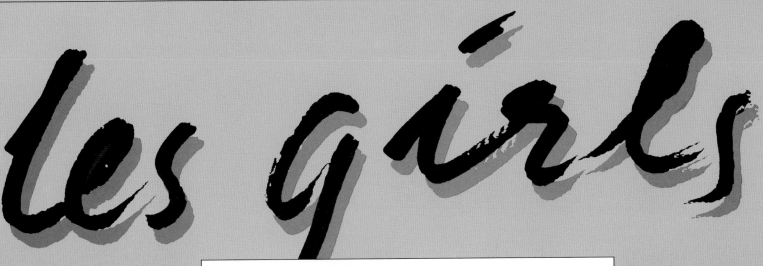

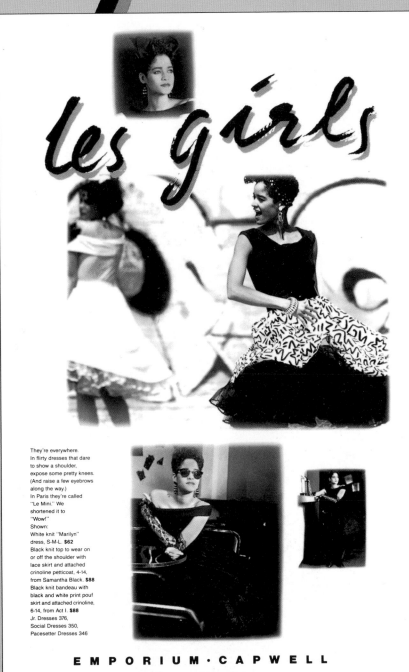

Terry Louie has projected a French-style attitude with his brush script and has made excellent use of it in this newspaper ad. The shadow effect is quite appropriate in this medium, which has limited printing capabilities. This piece was produced with art director Rawn McCloud for Emporium • Capwell.

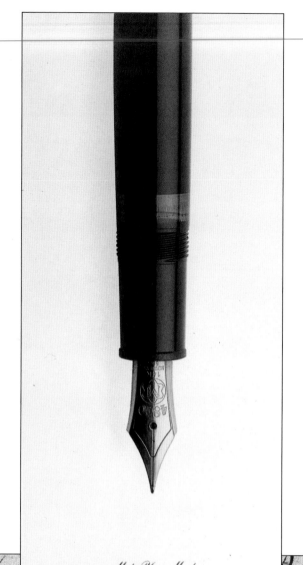

Georgia Deaver produced the calligraphic art for this promotional piece for Mead Paper Co. Designed by the Van Dyke Company with photography by Terry Heffernan, this work reflects the name of the paper being promoted, Signature from Mead. Her art conveys the impression both subjectively and literally of a multipurpose product, a perfect example of what can be achieved with the human hand.

Make Your Mark on Signature from Mead

Georgia contributed her talent to this literature piece *(top)* designed by Pate International for the Robert Mondavi Winery. The delicate lettering sits well within this subtle design. *Below,* in contrast, this bold announcement for the San Francisco Ballet brings to the dance program excitement and magic.

Sleeping Beauty
Tomasson (Petipa)/
Tchaikovsky/ Worsaae

New Full Length Production

World Premiere

J oin us this season as we add a sparkling new production of *Sleeping Beauty.* In celebration of the ballet's 100th anniversary, Helgi Tomasson and designer Jens-Jacob Worsaae, whose *Swan Lake* won critical acclaim, have once again joined forces to create a stunning new ballet which is sure to seize your imagination and capture your heart.

Sleeping Beauty represents the grandest achievement of classical ballet and offers thrilling bravura performances. From the romance of Princess Aurora and Prince Florimund's Pas de Deux to a colorful array of fairy tale characters, you won't want to miss this joyous experience of dance, music, and theatre. A delight for the whole family to cherish for all time. *Included on all 8 and 5 performance series, or order your individual tickets now!*

Sleeping Beauty
1990 Performance Dates

March

Sun	Mon	Tues	Wed	Thur	Fri	Sat
		13 8pm	**14** 8pm	**15** 8pm	**16** 8pm	
						24 2pm 8pm
25 2pm 7pm						

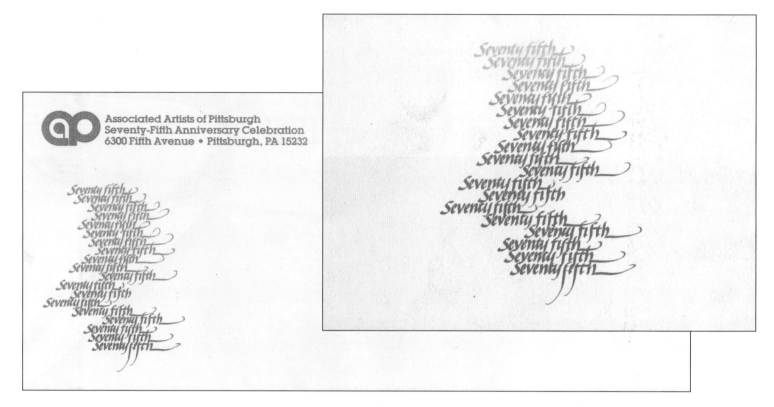

Joan Iversen Goswell of Valencia, Pennsylvania, has established free-form positioning of a repeated line on this invitation for an annual exhibition of the Associated Artists of Pittsburgh. She has combined this with a split-fountain effect to enhance the sense of movement.

Eliza Schulte has created this simple title for a clothing line that uses the image of jungle and animal patterns as a motif. This was produced with Paul Niski for Bullock's.

Julian Waters of Gaithersburg, Maryland, created this variety of calligraphic images to accompany a promotion for a series of U.S. commemorative stamps based on indigenous American animals. Following Terrence McCaffrey's direction and design, Julian handcrafted each name with a subjective attitude that resembles the animal it announces.

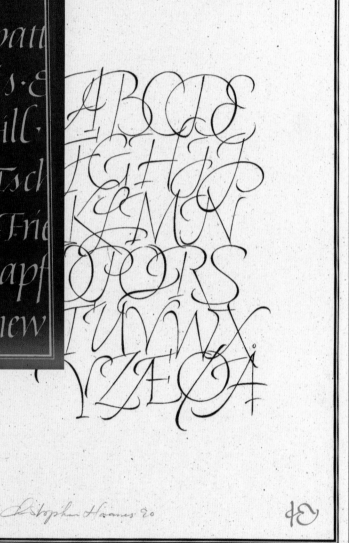

Christopher Haanes of Oslo, Norway, produced these images for a limited edition catalogue of fonts. *Top left,* a silkscreened front page. *Right,* an interior page showing one of the fonts. *Bottom left,* a stamp that was used as part of the presentation. This is beautifully crafted freehand lettering that has the look of pure art.

Georgia Deaver created the art spot on this convention folder *(top)* based on the theme of music manuscript. It was designed for the California Association of Hospitals & Health Systems and uses a delightful mix of colors. *Right,* a greeting card designed for Neugebauer Press using a different treatment of the same motif.

Julian Waters created these dramatic and colorful images for two folders concerning the benefits program at *The Washington Post* newspaper. They have such a strong and upbeat appearance that they inspire confidence and a real sense of security.

Packaging

The three designs on these two pages are the work of **Shigeru Akizuki** of Tokyo, Japan. He has beautifully matched the calligraphic backgrounds with the typography on these packages created for the Chintose Co. *Above,* containers of sweet bean jelly. *Top right,* a combination cake set. *Bottom right,* a combination package for baked Japanese round, brown buns. They prove that bold strokes *can* be subtle and persuasive.

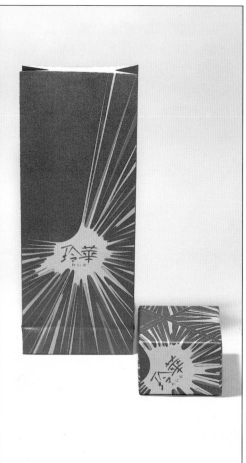

These three designs show the dynamic use of color and form that is evident in all the work of **Shigeru Akizuki**. From the split-font effect of mixing colors *(left)*, to the dramatic radiating lines *(center)*, to the bold embossed brushstrokes *(right)* he utilizes the appropriate amount of drama and effect to create a strong point-of-sale image without sacrificing the impression of quality.

This page displays containers and their packages and demonstrates how they can be successfully related. This is a common design problem in packaging, and Shigeru shows with these examples how the use of the freehand stroke is one excellent approach to a solution.

The Hanshin carry bags pictured here were designed by **Kenneth Willis Cato**. They show the effect of simple gesture art in just two colors. This is a striking example of simplicity in free form.

The handcrafted logotype and vignette of the Vienna skyline give this package for the European Common Market its distinct personality. This design by **Hans Flink** and **Jane Paraszczak** has found enormous success in Europe and has become a best-seller for the company.

These two applications of the same motif provide a colorful visual for a significant point-of-sale display. Designed by **Paul Beluk** for art director Mark Eckstein of the Berni Company, they prove the importance of being simple and direct when designing packaging for the quick-purchase retail market. Also the simple brushstroke makes it easy to connect all the different products with brand identification.

The wonderful use of color and free form makes this tag especially effective. Designed by **Peter Antipas** for the Berni Company as a logo for Elysian Fields, the brushstroke monogram works also as an eye-catching graphic and gives a sense of the quality of the product line and the market envisioned by the client.

In a combined effort, designer **Jim Hillis** and illustrator **Roger Lundquist** created this free-form rendering for Hillis Mackey & Co. The design uses the softness inherent in this graphic application to promote the nature of both the products and the expected results from using them.

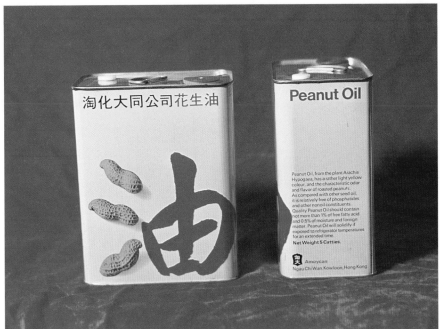

Henry Steiner designed this award-winning package for Amoy Peanut Oil. It is a striking example of the simple calligraphic form. The strong red over the clean white background combined with the free-floating peanuts makes for a whimsical and compelling image that captures the customer's interest.

Here are three wine labels created for Kenwood Vineyards as part of an Artist Series to promote their Sonoma Valley Cabernet Sauvignon. These labels present the ultimate graphic representation of fine art to define the quality and character of these wines. The top label has as its focus art by the 20th century painter **Joan Miro**. The label at lower left displays the work of artist/musician **Marcus Uzilevsky**, and lower right features the fine art of **Steve Jensen**.

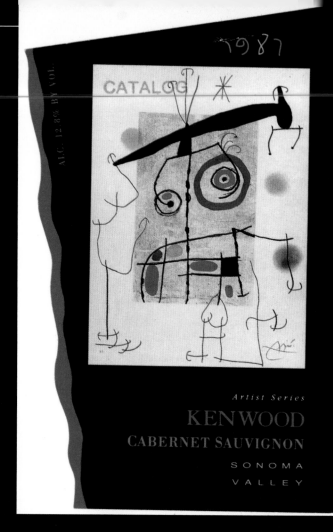

Carl S. Mazer has created these delightfully whimsical
wine labels for a series of gift wines for R.H. Macy & Co.,
Inc. What a fanciful departure this is from the seriousness
usually attributed to this product.

Tim Girvin of Seattle, Washington, has created these designs using different approaches to the freehand stroke. *Top*, a signature-like free flowing script for a carrying bag for the Simpson Co. *Bottom left*, a variety of scripts on a wine promotion. *Bottom right*, a wine label that incorporates a rough sketch-like image for a white table wine for Chateau Ste. Michelle Winery. This was specially created for Westin Hotels & Resorts.

Sherry Bringham of El Cerrito, California, has created this easy natural script for the California grape industry. She did this with art director Dave Devencenzi of DMBB.

Here is a nice combination of a basic san-serif typeface and a freehand script. **Brenda Walton** of Sacramento, California, with designer Cynthia Wulfsburg of Runyon Saltzman Weagraff Siegel created this shoppin bag for Arden Fair Mall.

The items on these two pages are label and package designs by **Primo Angeli**. He has created a sophisticated Bay Area look to the Just Right dessert package *(above)*. This contrasts noticeably with the Old West leather and gold effect he captured for the Wells Fargo Credit Corp. *(left)*. On the opposite page *(top)* Primo has suggested a gentle affirmation with these images for Shaklee Naturals Conditioning products. And finally, the much-admired Pete's Wicked Ale label and packaging *(opposite bottom)* that adds a bit of whimsy to the old brew.

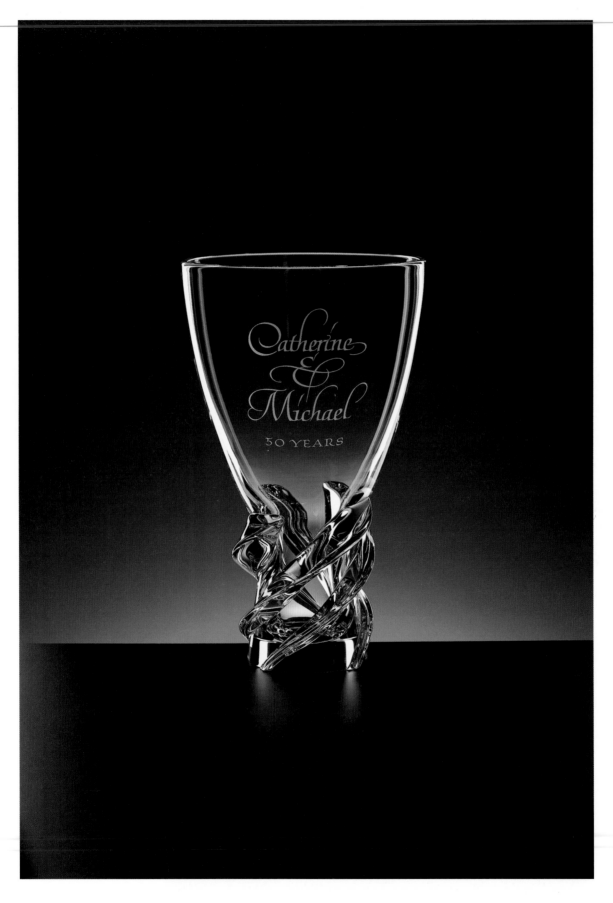

These two pages show an unexpected graphic use of
the brushstroke. **Patricia Weisberg** has created these
beautiful calligraphic images to be etched on crystal
glassware for Steuben Glass. Much of the freedom of
her originals is retained on the finished pieces, creating
an elegance and timelessness that's breathtaking.

The outline lettering for this series of wine coolers for Seagrams *(above)* was created by **Jane Dill** of San Francisco, California, to establish the concept of "Lightness." The word is superimposed over a soft airbrushed swatch of color to allow the white letter-forms to dominate while retaining their light effect. Michael Livolsi and Jack Vogler of Landor Associates, San Francisco designed these pieces to fully utilize the lettering. *Below,* a label for Black Mountain Spring Water, which won the 1st place Aqua Award from the International Bottled Water Association. Design firm: Addison/Olian Inc., art director: Mark Miyashiro.

Here **Joan Iversen Goswell** has created a gift package using very free calligraphic forms to illustrate the writing of Saen-Sa. The simple combination of color, design, and paper make this a moving visual experience.

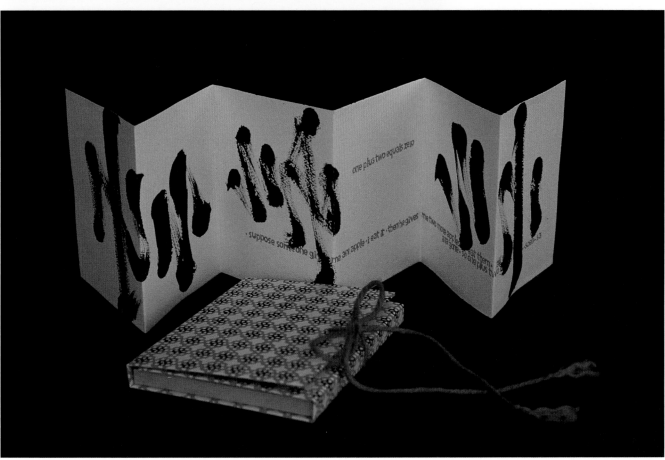

This is a classic use of the free script to give elegance and a sense of quality to a product, in this case Le Champ California Champagne. **Georgia Deaver** has used her special talents for this image, and the vertical placement of the name puts the finishing touch on a simple well-conceived design.

These packages of different Lavosh Hawaii flatbread products, with their sense of abundance and natural ingredients, carry the stylish freehand letterforms and art of **Larry Brady** of Los Alamitos, California. They were created with designer Bonnie Leah for Adrienne's Gormet Foods. Here is a strong combination of illustration and typography that makes a very compelling visual for the retail market.

Brenda Walton supplied the free-hand graphics for the product name on these containers of Fabergé Organics hair care products *(top)*. She worked with designer Susan Moriguchi of Landor Associates of New York to create this successful point-of-purchase image. *Bottom,* a lively appetite-inducing food image for Paragary's Pesto Pizza. Here she combined her work with designer Lila Wallrich of Gwen Amos Design of Sacramento, California, resulting in this design that is itself almost edible.

Covers & Posters

3

Brenda Walton has successfully created a graceful feminine script to title this book of short stories about women making life-changing decisions. It works well with the design of Barbara Fisher of Gospel Light Publications in presenting the feminine image to the reader.

These two posters also include Brenda's work. *Top,* a rough-edged script compliments the image of "Nostalgia" created by designer Tim Cummings of Cummings & Associates, Stockton, California. *Below,* with designer Michelle Weatherbee of Broom & Broom, San Francisco, California, she has developed this modern version of the classic script for the words "Be the Best" on this poster for Industrial Indemnity.

On two of these covers *Top and lower left,* **Tim Girvin** has used the quick brush-stroke as an illustrative device that is very much in keeping with the concept of this book. Both the delicate freeform flower and the bold dollar sign depict the attitudes of the accompanying texts and contribute subjectively to the designs. *Below, right,* a cover for *Inc.* magazine with a strong use of color and design.

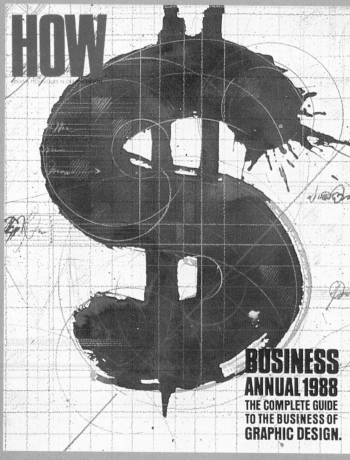

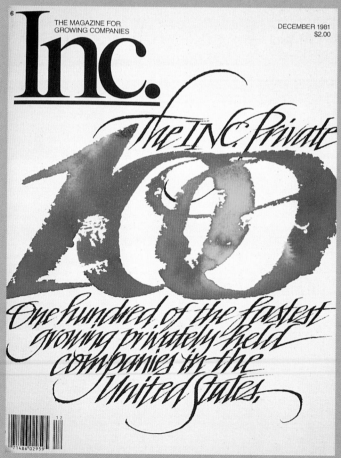

Here Tim has joined forces with designer Judy Arisman of Essex, Massachusetts, on these two covers for Houghton-Mifflin. *Top,* a lively calligraphic piece that is self-explanatory in its style. *Below,* another illustrative use of the quick brush-stroke to carry the message of the title.

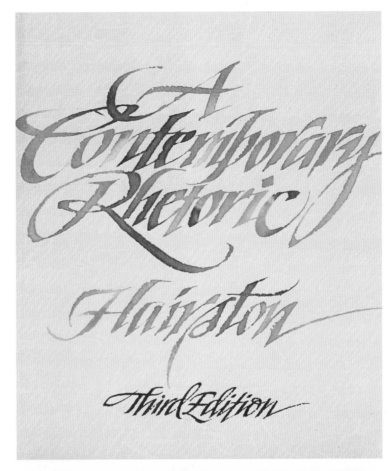

Here **Paul Shaw** has utilized his ability to produce many styles of lettering to create a relevant background texture for this cover of *Meetings & Conventions* magazine. The texture seems alive and full of connected movement and the colors enhance the overall effect of a handcrafted piece. There is also a positive tension established between the obvious handwork and the bold typography of the magazine title.

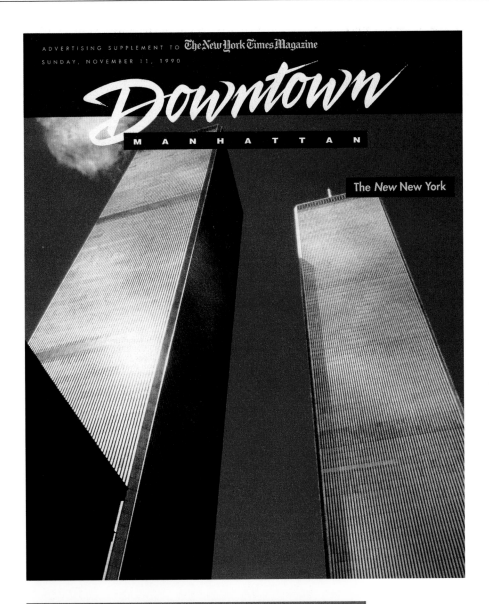

Anthony Block created the script for *The New York Times' Downtown Manhattan* cover. Its purpose was to promote downtown businesses in the World Trade Center. He enhanced the rough brush endings to give them their spontaneous feeling.

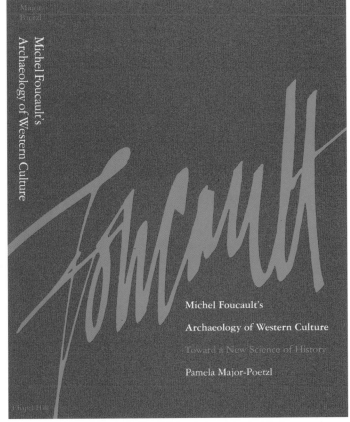

This book jacket, done for The University of North Carolina Press, Chapel Hill, uses the calligraphy of **Jean Evans** to give the bold effect of an enlarged signature. This one word carries the entire design and makes a strong impact on the potential reader.

The story headlines on these covers were created by **John Stevens** and are excellent examples of the use of the freehand for topical situations in news magazines. In each case the title uniquely portrays the subject matter of the lead story and becomes a strong invitation to pursue the article inside. *Top left,* created with Peter Comittini; *top right,* with Mark Inglis; *bottom,* with Ina Saltz.

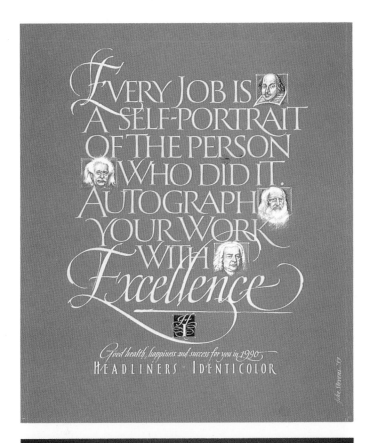

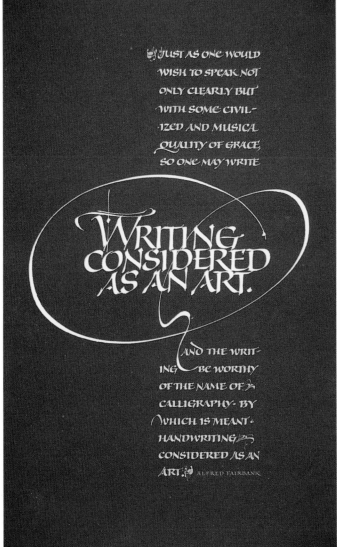

John has created a seasonal promotion *(top)* for Headliners/Identi-color by combining his calligraphy with small art spots as a form of story-telling graphics. *Below,* a poster promoting the art of calligraphy using text from Alfred Fairbank.

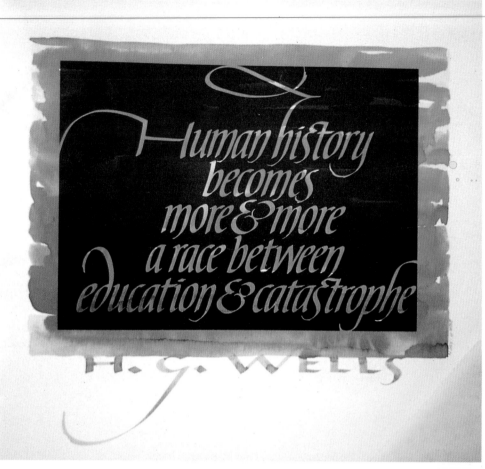

Above are two covers by **Nancy Culmone** of
Littleton, Massachusetts. *Top,* a cover for *T.H.E.
Journal* using an H. G. Wells quote as content.
Below, an Acton/Boxborough Interaction catalog
cover with the word "Interaction" rendered in
script overprinting a bold abstraction of the same
word.

These two pieces of line art, also created by Nancy Culmone, are inspirational pieces that show how well freehand art works as descriptive and illustrative material for communication.

The cover pictured above is an excellent example of the combination of letterforms and illustration. The free penwork of the title by **Gun Larson** of Sweden works perfectly with the illustration by Jack Standish to give the atmosphere of time and reflection, which is the core of this philosophical book.

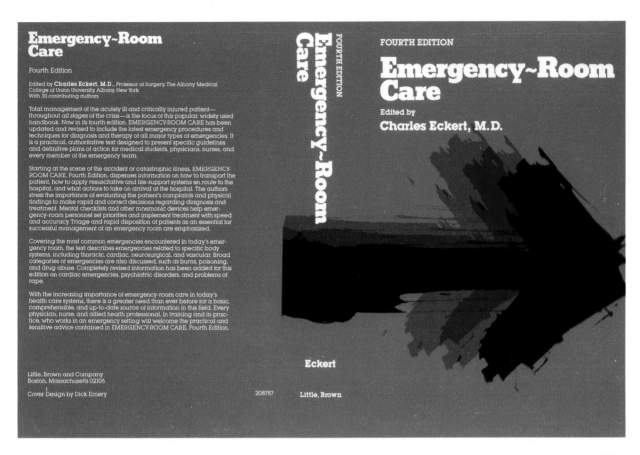

The two paperback covers shown above illustrate how free brushwork can capture the mood or attitude of a book without being the actual letterforms of the title. *Top,* **Richard Emery** uses the bold dramatic brushstroke to project the sense of emergency. *Bottom,* he uses the very free abstract brush image to convey the freedom of expression in linguistics. These books, designed for Little, Brown and Co., are prime examples of how abstraction can carry the message.

Once again **Mike Quon** has used his quick
brush skills *(above)* to create humor and
directness. Each of these magazine covers
carries a sense of appropriate levity that
deals directly with the content. To the left is
a wonderful example of the use of excess
in flourish and swash to gain an other-
worldly effect. This piece was done with
steel pens and Chinese stick ink by **Gun
Larson** for a Pantheon book jacket.

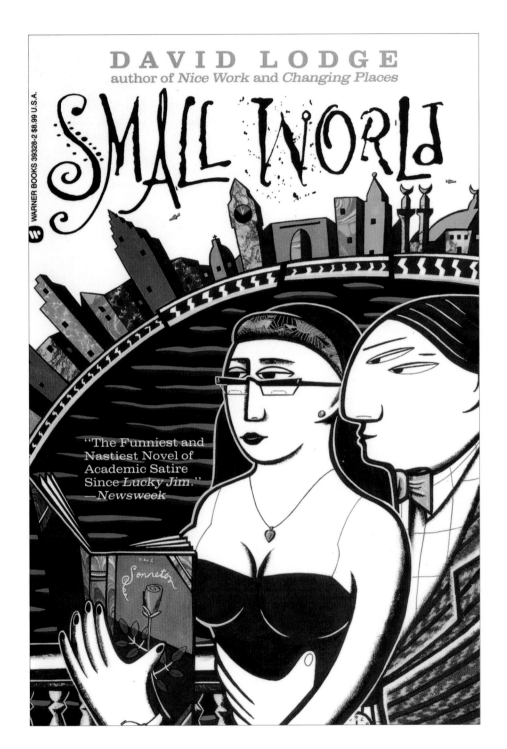

Here is a combination of calligraphy by **Bernard Maisner** and artwork by Ed Miliano that was submitted by art director Jackie Meyer of Warner Books. This piece projects the image of humor and satire and accomplishes what all good art should in setting the tone of a book.

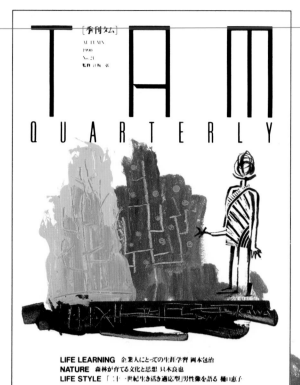

Here is a childlike, quick brush piece that follows the basic concept of this book by its simple and direct approach. Though it is illustrative in nature, it still fulfills the objective of spontaneity and subjective expression. **Hideyuki Kawarasaki** created this cover art for designer Masai Kei for *TAM Quarterly*.

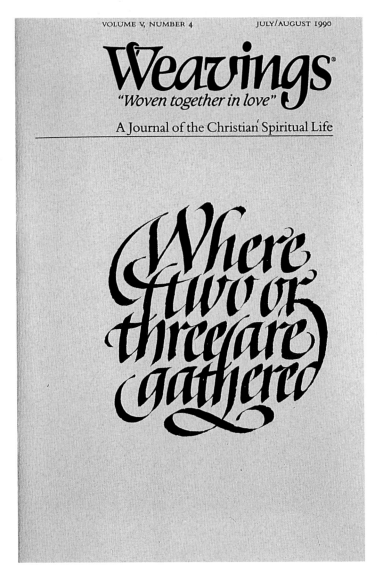

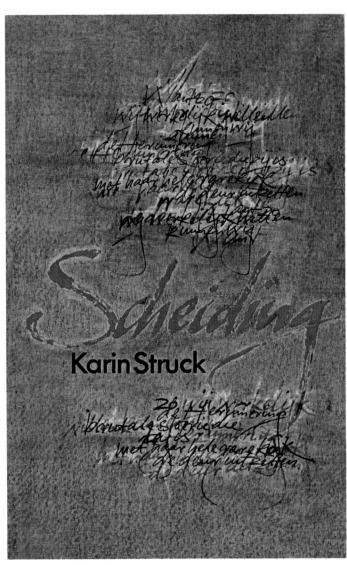

Paul Shaw produced this cover art on Fabriano watercolor paper for art director Nelson Kane of *Weavings* magazine.

This cover was created in "fine art" style by **Karina Meister** of The Netherlands for Grote ABC Books. It shows how beautiful and subjective art can carry the message.

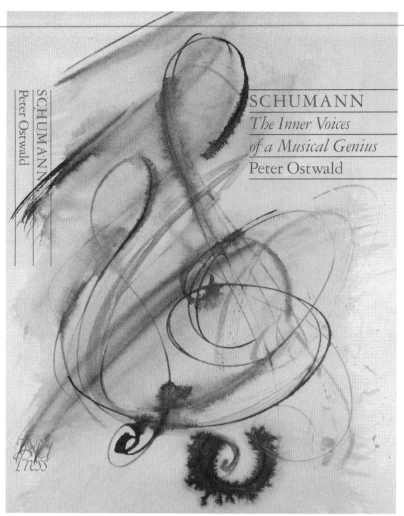

This is a very free treatment of line and wash. **Jean Evans** created this art for designer Janice Wheeler for Northeastern University Press. The art portrays the musical genius yet unstable personality of this nineteenth century composer.

Right, the front cover of a menu for Pan Am created by **Ivan Chermayeff**. The marvelous texture of the pen lines combined with the color spots produces a pattern that projects the worldwide nature of this airline.

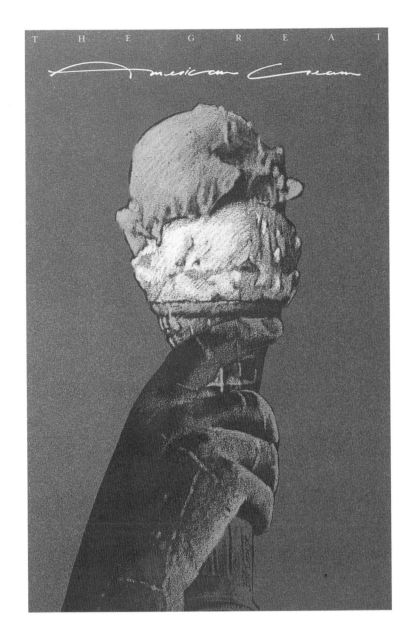

Bob Conge has designed some very imaginative posters. Here are two pieces that combine strong illustrative art with calligraphic headlines. Both the Great American Cream poster and the 1987 Park Avenue Arts Festival poster combine the sense of tradition with a modern graphic approach that is delightful and evocative.

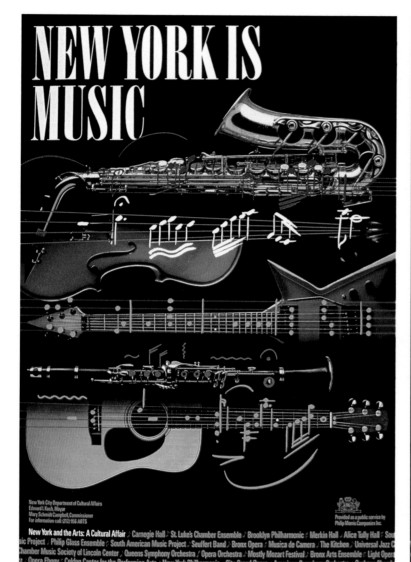

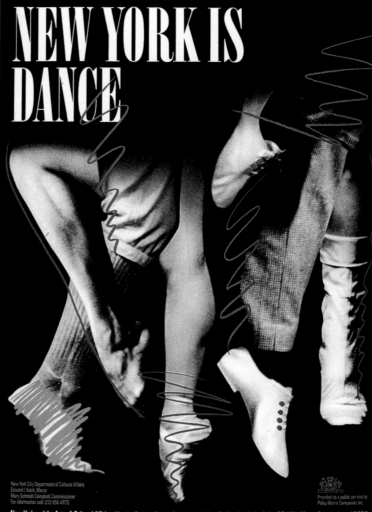

These three posters *(this page and the opposite page, left)* are excellent examples of the use of multi-image design. **Steff Geissbuhler** has combined photography, art, and freehand graphics to produce these stunning posters — *New York is . . . Music, Dance, Theater.* They successfully depict the high level of art that is found in New York City by the very nature and quality of their own presentation. Each poster has relied heavily on the use of color and drama to carry the graphics to their highest level.

In keeping with the New York City theme, here is a bilingual cultural poster. **Chee Wang Ng**, calligrapher, and Guo-Ping Zhang, designer, have used the juxtaposition of the calligraphic form and the dynamic figure to retain the strong Chinese identity.

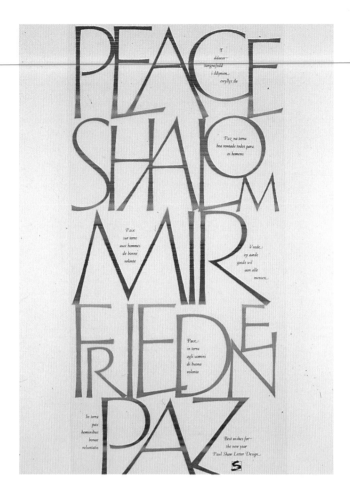

These three inspirational poster-style images were designed by **Paul Shaw**. They show not only artistic integrity but also a real sensitivity to the messages. The Peace design was printed in 5 colors with handset typography. The Work poster was rendered with a ruling pen on paper for art director Rochelle Arthur. And finally, the Go and Show design was produced for the Methodist Church and art director Nelson Kane.

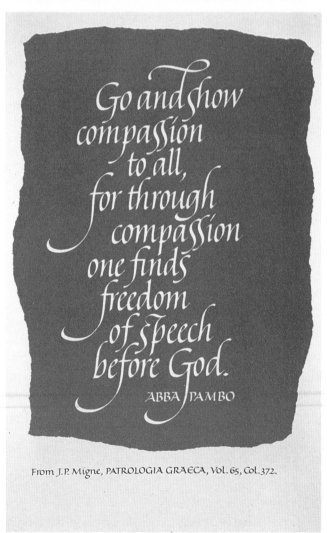

Also by **Paul Shaw**, this exhibition poster is for a show of his own calligraphic art at Long Island University. Not only are the letterforms well conceived but so is their placement together. The reverse white letterforms show off the rough-stroked edges well and give a dynamic punch to the whole piece.

The three pieces of design on these two pages display the bold and vibrant approach of **Denise Foreman** of Sidney, Australia. They show her expansive style of brushwork with an emphasis on strong primary colors as an accompaniment. On this page *(top)* is a magazine cover, *The Hollywood Reporter*, designed for the Beyond International Group. The imagery is quite appropriate to the subject. *Below*, is a T-shirt design to promote a comedy duo, *Club Veg*, on radio in Sidney. It surely gives the impression that the listener is in for an experience of wild and wacky humor.

Above we have a colorful sweatshirt design she produced for Virgin Records to celebrate the Bicentenary in Sidney. The obvious atmosphere of festivity and celebration leaps out from this delightful piece, and we sense a demonstration of pride in the city it honors.

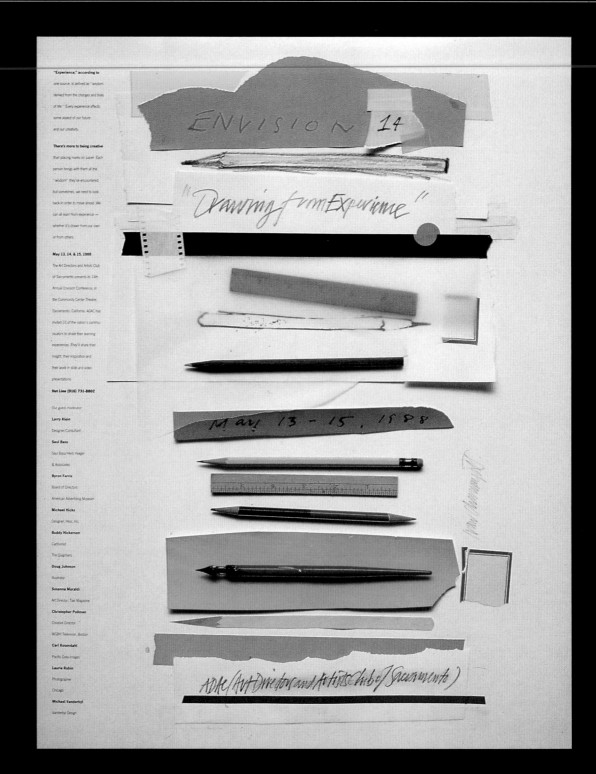

Ivan Chermayeff designed this *Envision Conference* poster for the Art Directors and Artists Club of Sacramento. Since it was promoting a conference on art, the imagery is compelling, and the pen/pencil strokes establish a relationship with the remaining typography that conveys the high level of this conference.

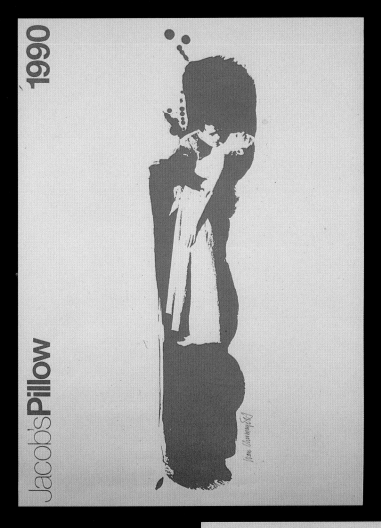

These three posters for the Jacob's Pillow Dance Company are also the work of Ivan Chermayeff. Here he has successfully incorporated the realism of dance images within freely rendered brushstrokes. These images clearly portray the excitement, the form, and the beauty that this company generates.

Here **Paul Shaw** has designed a strong, stylized calligraphic poster to promote *Brooklyn Accents 2*, an annual celebration of Brooklyn literature, journalism, and dramatic arts. Using the letterforms to simulate handwritten signatures gives this poster the feeling of creative writing and literature.

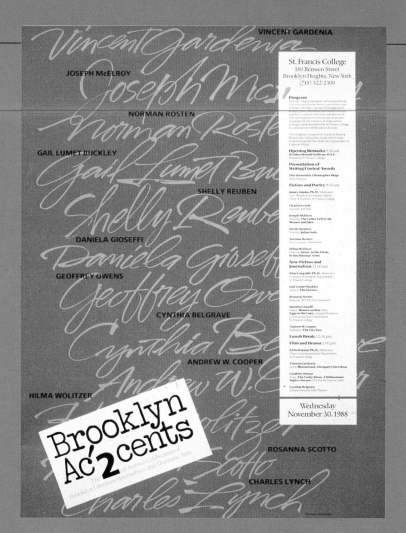

Susan Skarsgard designed this poster for the AIGA. This extraordinary use of line and texture fits so well with the headline about writing.

Karina
Meister

Ignaz
Günther
Haus des
Münchner
Stadtmuseums

St.-Jakobs-Platz 15

13. Juli bis
12. August 1984

Öffnungszeiten:
Dienstag mit Samstag 9 bis 16.30 Uhr,
Sonntag 10 bis 18 Uhr

Here is another example of the successful use of calligraphy as a background texture. **Karina Meister** of The Netherlands created the art for this exhibition poster with a clear idea of matching the detail and free texture with the simple sans serif typography accompanying it.

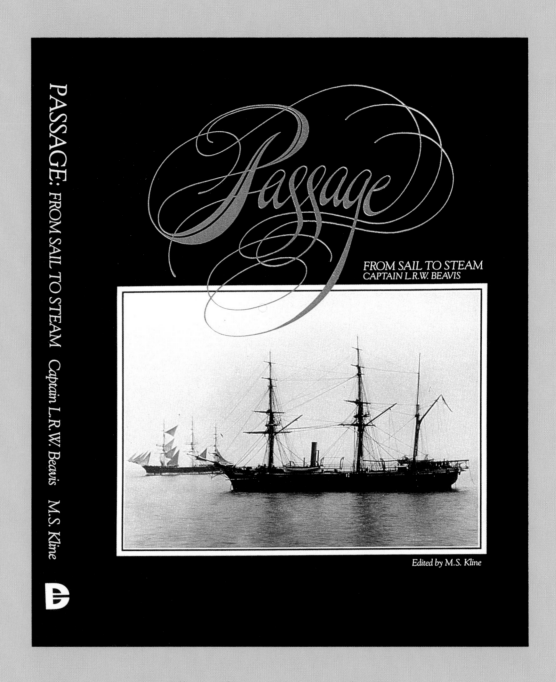

Dia Calhoun of Seattle, Washington, designed this jacket for a book about the passage from sail to steam. It was created in conjunction with the 100th anniversary of the city of Vancouver and has the look of great historical style and significance. The use of silver foil on the script lettering is not insignificant in giving this visual its sense of permanence.

Dia created this image *(left)* for a poster promoting a publication of the opera *Aida* as told by Leontyne Price. It was produced for Harcourt Brace Jovanovich, Publishers. Again, the use of silver is deliberate and enhances the illustration by Leo and Diane Dillon. *Right,* a poster announcing the production of a play at the West Seattle Totem Theatre. She combined with Rollin Thomas to create this uneasy and provocative image.

The calligraphy on this poster by **Rose Folsom** works well with the design of Pieter Arend Folkens and the illustration of Charlotte C. Carlisle. This piece has a wonderful range of graphic applications including two different varnishes.

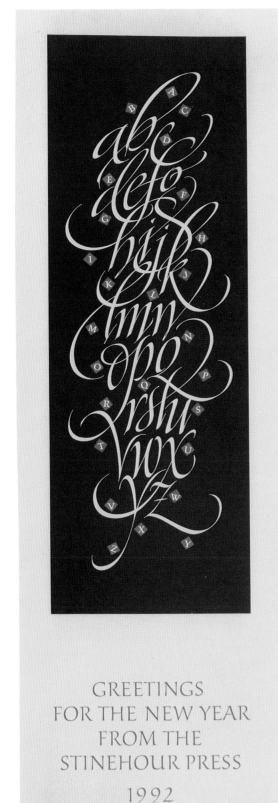

GREETINGS
FOR THE NEW YEAR
FROM THE
STINEHOUR PRESS
1992

Here are three examples of the work of **Julian Waters** showing the great diversity of his talent. *Left,* a seasonal greetings poster that he designed for The Stinehour Press. *Top right,* a poster for Kalamazoo College, Michigan, which includes his calligraphy and the fanciful design and illustration of Becky Huber-Van Zoeren. *Bottom right,* a poster invitation for an opinion survey at IBM using a great mixture of color and textured line.

JOHN
Steinbeck

Warren French

Gabriel García
MÁRQUEZ

Raymond Williams

NATHANIEL
Hawthorne

Terence Martin

JEAN · PAUL
Sartre

Catharine Savage Brosman

Eugene
O'Neill

Frederick I. Carpenter

VIRGINIA
Woolf

Susan Rubinow Gorsky

T. S. Eliot

Philip R. Headings

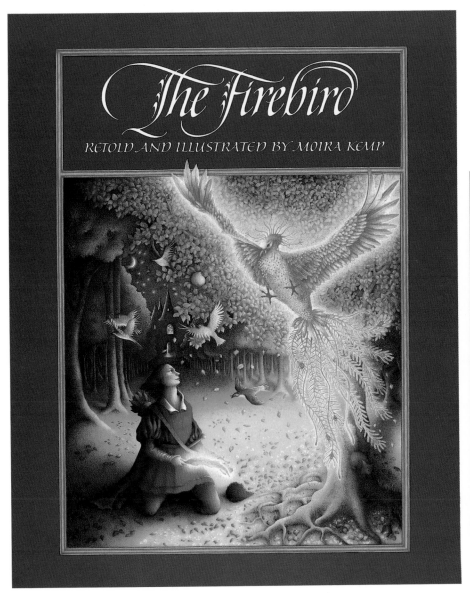

These two pages show the work of **Richard Lipton** of Dorchester, Massachusetts. *Opposite,* a series of book covers concerning literary personalities where he has matched up different styles of lettering with the names, giving diversity within a series look. On this page   *(left)* his flowing script works well with the illustration by Moira Kemp of this traditional Russian fairy tale published by David R. Godine Publisher. *Right,* a book title and author also for Godine.

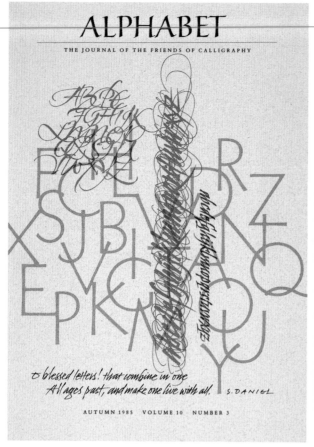

Here are three pieces by **Rick Cusick**. The top two show quite different approaches to the same basic image. *Top left,* a group of overprinting images for a journal cover with a masthead by John Prestianni. *Top right,* a keepsake given at a lecture for the New York Society of Scribes. It's interesting how well the same image works in each design. *Right,* a delicate line illustration of initials enhances a poster advertising an exhibition of his work.

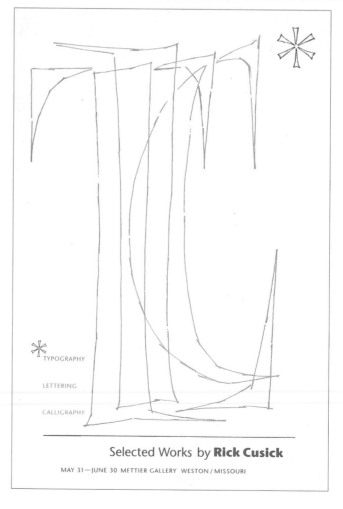

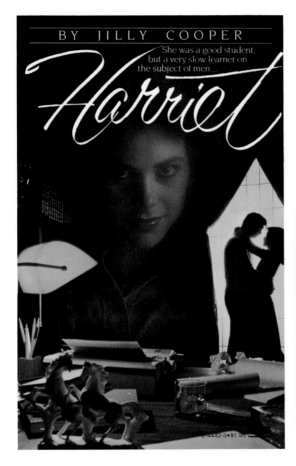

Edward Vartanian has done many titles for book covers and films. Here are three that show his stylistic range. *Top left,* a cover for a Fawcett Crest Fiction series. *Top right,* a bold graffiti-like film title that lurches at the viewer. *Lower left,* a title for a George Cornell book cover.

Sherry Bringham has her own
versatile approach to freehand
brushwork, and the pieces on these
two pages demonstrate that. *Top,* a
poster for the Louis Martini Winery,
including a detail enlargement of her
strong brushstroke. *Bottom,* a poster
celebrating the 50th anniversary of
the Golden Gate Bridge created for
Henri's Top of the Hilton. *Opposite,*
two pages from a calendar for the
Graphic Arts of Marin, each quite
different in style and appearance.

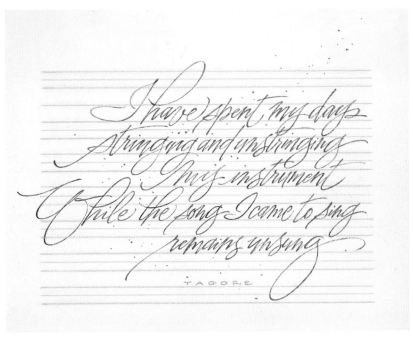

Three examples of the work of **Carl Rohrs** of Santa Cruz, California, appear on these two pages. *Opposite,* a marvelous poster-calendar designed by Sutherland Design with photography by Thomas Burke and calligraphy by Carl. This image has a sculptural effect even to the letterforms themselves and is a very successful use of calligraphy within illustration. *Top,* a poster announcing a peace event combining Carl's calligraphy with the art of John Babcock. *Below,* a piece promoting and celebrating handmade brushes.

Right, a cover design for Drewry Lane Bookmakers and Publishers by **Joey Hannaford** of Atlanta, Georgia, that sings just like the title. *Below,* a Charles Dickens reprint created with Robin Wineman for Larry Smith & Associates.

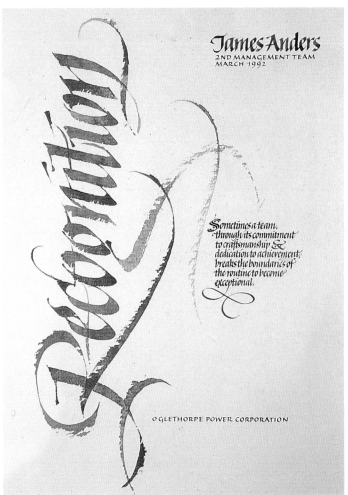

Here *(top left)* Joey has created a poster celebrating the words of Ramakrishna with a strong design of earth colors and letterforms. *Top right,* a recognition award for the Oglethorpe Power Corp., and a cheery upbeat "Get Well" card designed for the Crawford Long Hospital of Atlanta *(bottom).*

Colleen of Brookline, Massachusetts, shows her unique talent on these two pages starting with the cover title *(top)* that she created for art director Susan Lu of Little, Brown and Company. *Below left,* a promotion for the Essex Institute and its 300th anniversary; Dawn Rogola, art director. *Below right,* a T-shirt and poster promotion created with Pam Hess as art director for a Pan-Mass. Challenge bike ride for the Jimmy Fund.

THE SALEM WITCH TRIALS OF 1692

The Reebok Human Rights Program
Recognizes

Bonnie Raitt

When good people do nothing,
evil triumphs;
when good people take a stand,
everything becomes possible –
including freedom.
We honor your readiness
to use your gifts to further the cause
of human rights,
and we commend your devotion
to extending the boundaries of freedom.

Paul Fireman
Chairman & CEO Reebok International Ltd.

Jimmy Carter
39th President, United States of America

Here Colleen joined with Sue
Nappi of Nappi Design to
create this Reebok Award
(top) combining the art and
letterforms in dramatic
fashion. *Bottom,* an imaginative poster designed for Susan
Courtemanche of the Worcester Art Museum, Worcester,
Massachusetts.

Combining with Ken Krause of Creative Design & Marketing, **Bonnie Spiegel** developed this poster *(top)* for a gift promotion for Fleet Bank, a nice typographic balance. *Below,* a bumper sticker for WBLM Radio created for Bruce Harrison Design. This brushwork shouts its intended message at you.

Bonnie has created a startling freehand image for this book cover designed for The Cumberland Press. The lettering and art graphically depict the horror of the book's content.

THE
SAN FRANCISCO
SYMPHONY
1990-91 SEASON

HERBERT BLOMSTEDT
MUSIC DIRECTOR

The work on this spread represents the collaborations of calligrapher **Jane Dill**. *Left,* with art director Diane Levin of Design Resource, a piece for the San Francisco Symphony. *Below,* with designer Sharon Till, a cover for the Sterling Winery. *Opposite top,* also with Sharon Till, a promotion for Classic Hawaiian Holidays. *Bottom left,* with Linda Herman of Herman & Co., a cover for Chronicle Books, San Francisco, and, with Dean Seven, a magazine cover for *FAD Magazine*, San Francisco *(bottom right).*

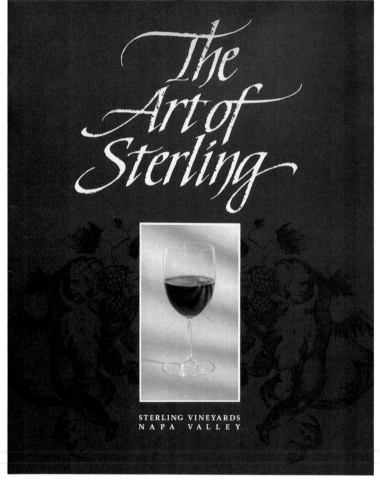

Classic Values

14 Exceptional Hawaiian Vacation Values for 1990

TALES OF A
SINGLE MOTHER

ADAIR LARA

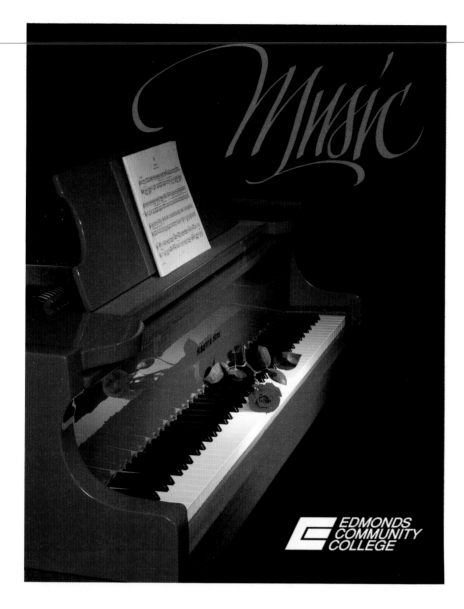

Jocelyn Curry of Seattle, Washington, created this moody cover for a literature piece about the music department of Edmonds Community College, Lynnwood, Washington.

Claude Dieterich A. of Miami Beach, Florida, has created with his stylish lettering this travel image for the cruise liner *M/V Bucanero*.

Claude Dieterich A. also has produced this powerful theater poster *(left)* with its strong use of color and handcrafted imagery. *Below,* a catalog cover for a Peruvian art exhibition.

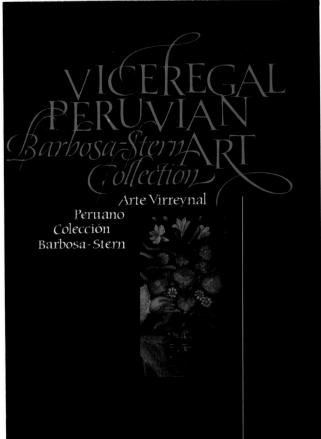

Fritz Eberhardt of Schwenksville, Pennsylvania, has created these beautifully calligraphed posters containing excerpts from the writings of Shakespeare. They are being sold in gift shops and theater shops. The calligraphic style both in the letterforms and the illustration serves the bard well and makes them valuable gift items.

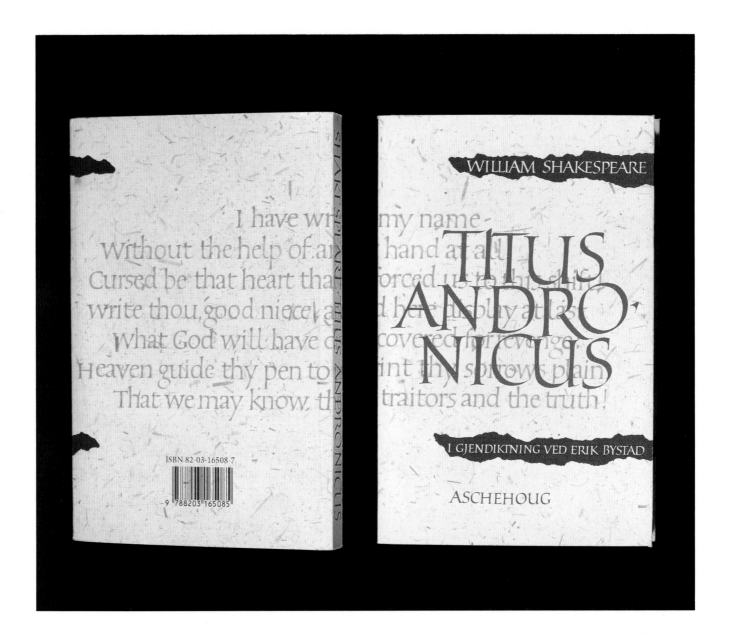

Christopher Haanes has created this book cover for art
director Kristian Ystehede, Aschehoug, Norway. It has the
classical attitude appropriate to it and is beautiful in its use
of texture, color, and overlapping.

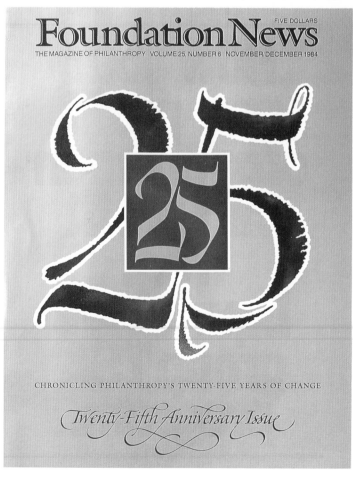

Top, **Julian Waters** created the cover image for this literature piece for the American Association of Retired Persons by using the spectrum color scheme on his letterforms. *Below,* the cover image for the 25th anniversary issue of the magazine *Foundation News* with similar multi-colored typography, this time over a silver metallic background.

Below, the cover for the program schedule for an annual meeting of the National Association of Convenience Stores. The bright colors combined with Julian's lettering give this piece its appropriate tropical atmosphere. *Right,* the cover for a booklet describing the Postal Services' commemorative stamps.

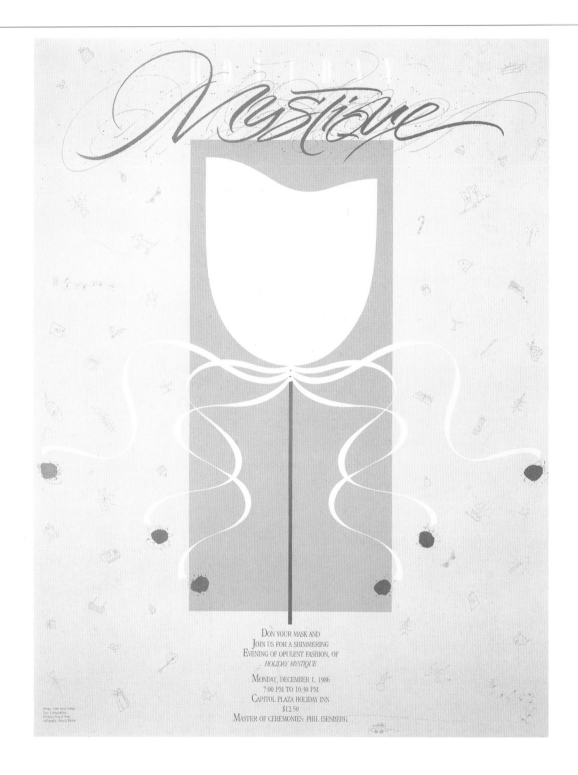

Here is a poster that **Brenda Walton** has
applied her calligraphic talent to. It was
created by Gwen Amos Design, Sacramento,
California, for South Area Emergency Housing.
Muted pastel colors were added to Brenda's
lettering to create this "Mystique" effect. Lila
Wallrich was the designer.

Corporate ID

In designing this corporate image for Serono-Baker Diagnostics, **Rose Farber,** senior art director at Lewis & Grace, chose to introduce the brushstroke of the logo in a pre-launch mailer *(top)*. This was a preliminary exposure to the graphic design that would eventually be in the corporate image *(bottom)*. This is an example of a free stroke accommodating both the actual logo design and the general overall image that the company intended to present throughout its design program.

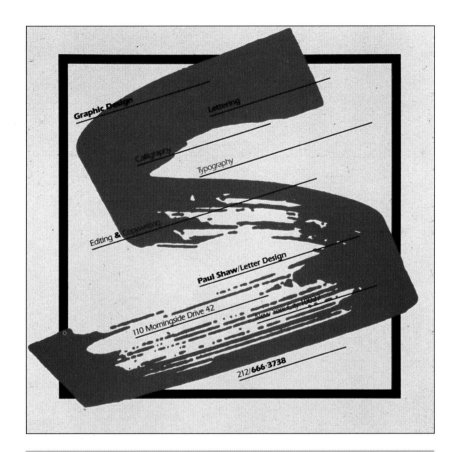

With Bouwsma pens and homemade ink **Paul Shaw** created this logo for his own company, Paul Shaw/Letter Design. Here is a self promotion piece that balances its bold free texture with the clean lines of the basic typography, Eras. This image leaves little doubt concerning the nature and excitement of the artist's work.

This design, created as the logo for the Lipton Championships tennis events in Key Biscayne, Florida, cleverly uses the different elements to depict more than single images. **Jim Williams** has used the brushstroke to simulate both a palm tree and a tennis racquet. Likewise, the bold-line tennis ball is also the image of the sun in the sky.

FAUVE FASHION

 HAND PAINTED ORIGINALS / 1 FAIRFAX RD, MOSMAN,
SYDNEY, AUSTRALIA, 2088. TEL: (02) 9604550

Here **Denise Foreman** of Sydney,
Australia, has created a logo and
company image for Fauve Fashion, a
company that creates hand-painted
original designs. The image directly
addresses the freehand nature of their
product and establishes the quality they
represent.

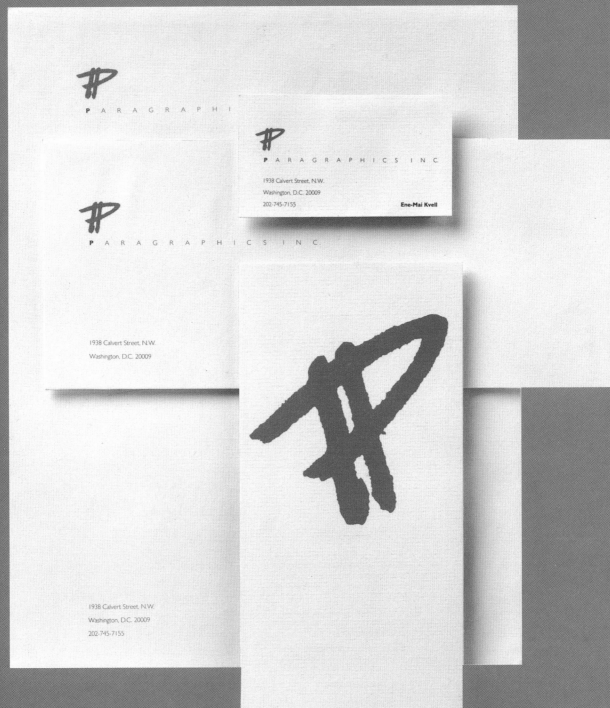

Gayle Monkkonen designed this corporate image/logo for Paragraphics Inc. It is extremely effective in combining the heavy brushstroke with the delicate lines of typography. Pictured here are letterhead, envelope, calling card and cover of a literature piece.

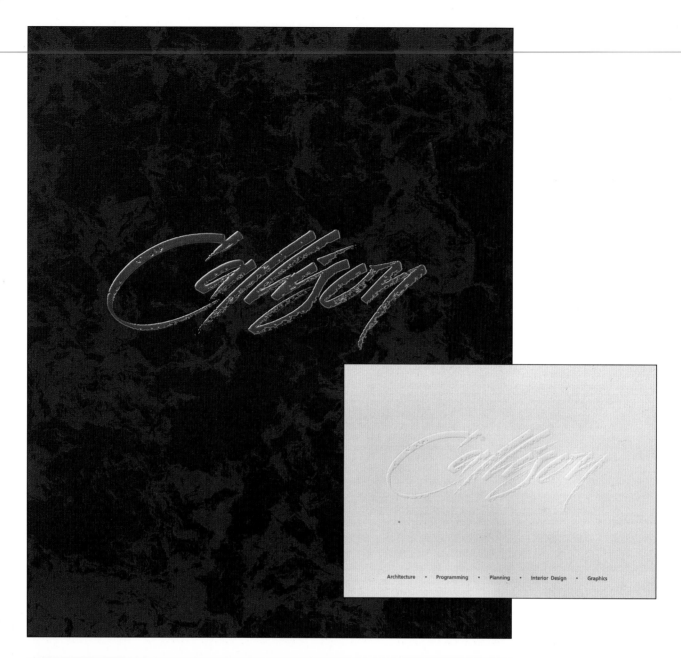

On this page, two designs by **Iskra Johnson**. *Top,* this piece shows the possibilities of freehand brush with the technique of embossing. Created for the Callison design firm, the logo on the larger piece was first printed in a copper metallic ink and then embossed. The smaller piece is raised embossing on white paper. The lower design (Koalas) shows a single color wash treatment of a logo created for Anheuser-Busch and Busch Gardens.

Here is a promotional sheet showing the freehand capabilities of
Thomas Carnase. These examples show the wide range of
expression he has used for a number of prominent clients in
establishing their logos and identification marks.

Anthony Bloch has created this ID spot for a promotional campaign for the artist Theadius McCall. The campaign included posters to be carried in shopping bags, rolled up and fastened with a blue ribbon.

Henry Less Productions Inc. 1196 Queen Street West, Toronto, Ontario M6J 1J6

Henry Less Productions Inc.
1196 Queen Street West
Toronto, Ontario M6J 1J6
(416) 532-1116

Henry Less Productions Inc. 1196 Queen Street West, Toronto, Ontario M6J 1J6 • (416) 532-1116

This corporate image was designed for Henry Less Productions Inc. of Toronto, Ontario, by **Rowennie Cheng** of Bowen Designs, Inc., and displays a strong use of color and freehand.

Kenneth Willis Cato, of Victoria, Australia, has designed the four pieces on these two pages. *Top left,* a bold single initial monogram logo for Revelations Shoe Company, USA. Its strength and simplicity projecting from the dark red background make it very recognizable for repeat identification. *Below left,* a promotion piece for Vega Press addressing their use of color. Here the brush graphics take on both the image of flowers and swabs of printing ink.

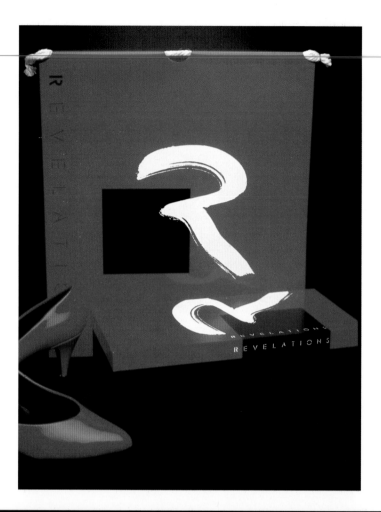

Above, a design piece he
created for the Graphic Arts
Service Association of
Australia (GASA). It inte-
grates the freehand sketch of
a letter form with other
symbols of the graphics
industry. *Below,* a stationery
range for Fullstop.

Once again, here is a wonderful use of embossing as a vehicle for the free stroke. **Bob Conge**, a graphic designer and illustrator, has created this work for his own studio image. There is a nice visual exchange between the grey textured paper and the raised embossing.

RICHARD EMERY DESIGN, INC. 79 Eastern Ave., Essex, MA 01929
768-6510

RICHARD EMERY DESIGN, INC. 79 Eastern Ave., Essex, MA 01929
768-6510

Pictured here is a simple
one-color logotype that
forms the image of a
graphic design studio.
Richard Emery created
this logo to generate a
sense of vitality and
energy. This, he believes
best represents his studio
and the work that they
produce.

Henry Steiner, of Graphic Communication Ltd, Hong Kong, has designed these three logos with a definite Oriental cast to them. The design for IBM World Trade Asia Corporation *(top)* has the virgule between the A and P appropriately rendered with a brushstroke. The design for Jade Creations Ltd, *(middle)* a jewelry manufacturer, has the letter 'E' replaced by the Chinese character for 'jade'. The Yale Club of Hong Kong is a university alumni club. Its logo *(bottom)* gives the idea of a synthesis of east and west by combining straight blue lines (the Yale color) with authentic black calligraphic brushstrokes.

Ruth Pettis of St. Petersburg, Florida, has
taken a sketchy, handcrafted approach for
this logo spot for James Tapley Book-
binder. The combination of this freehand
lettering with the textured paper creates a
wonderful sense of the history and timelessness of this profession.

Caledonian
Landscaping

Suite 110
1417 East 8th Ave
Vancouver, BC
Canada V5N 1T3
604/879.9199

Caledonian
Landscaping

PO Box 80251
South Burnaby,
British Columbia
Canada V5H 3X5

Caledonian
Landscaping

PO Box 80251
South Burnaby,
British Columbia
Canada V5H 3X5
604/439.3110

Kevin Danner

Raymond Mah of
RayMahDesign, Inc. created
this piece for Caledonian
Landscaping. There is a
sensitive combination of
elements here that make this
concept work well. The
simulation of the plant form
with the brushstrokes
combines with both the
colors and the paper stock
to project a truly organic
image.

Trevenen
Apparel Ltd

5365 Headland Dr.
Caulfeild Village
Shopping Centre
West Vancouver, BC
Canada V7W 3C7

Telephone
604/926.1213

Trevenen
Apparel Ltd

5365 Headland Dr.
Caulfeild Village
Shopping Centre
West Vancouver, BC
Canada V7W 3C7

Anthony Trevenen Willett

Trevenen
Apparel Ltd

5365 Headland Dr.
Caulfeild Village
Shopping Centre
West Vancouver, BC
Canada V7W 3C7

Telephone
604/926.1213

Trevenen
Apparel Ltd

5365 Headland Dr.
Caulfeild Village
Shopping Centre
West Vancouver, BC
Canada V7W 3C7

Telephone
604/926.1213

Also created by **Raymond Mah** is this ID
spot for Trevenen Apparel Ltd. Here he has
designed a sophisticated image that speaks
not only of texture and fabric, but also of
pattern and design. There is a wonderful
use of the white space surrounding the
design in each of the examples. While each
piece is treated separately, all of them bear
the same design approach and identification.

Here is a series of three logo designs created by **Minoru Morita**. Each of these designs has its own distinct signature, and yet bears the unique touch of the designer. *Top right,* this design was produced for the Creative Center Inc. It makes use of another technique that works well with the free brushstroke, the implied shadow. *Lower right,* the corporate design for his own studio, Minoru Morita Graphic Design. Here the vertical freestrokes create an optical illusion that represents the identifying initial. *Lower left,* a free-spirited logo designed for M Design Associates. It has established, through quick spontaneous brush-strokes, the image of crashing waves and an energy that is forever in motion.

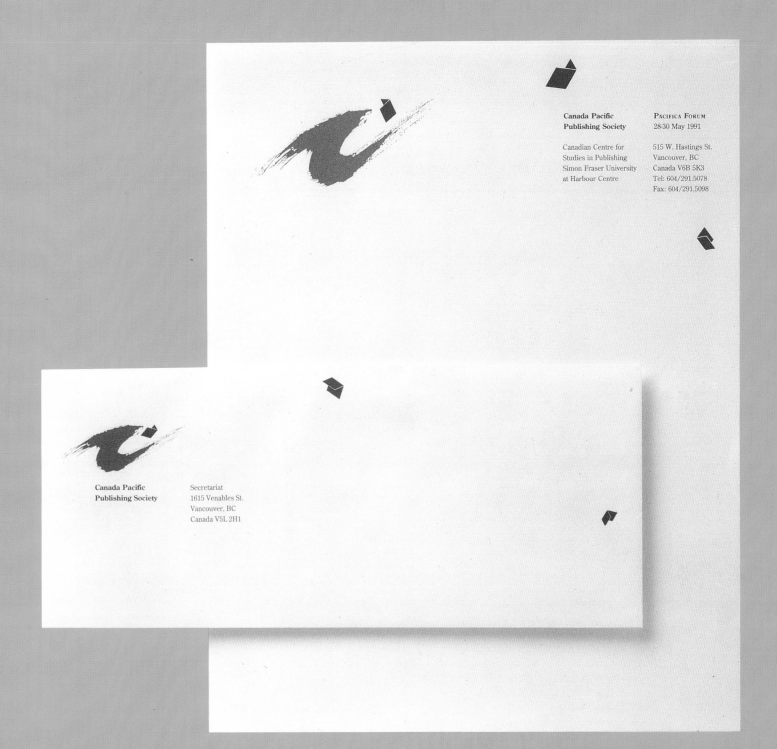

Canada Pacific
Publishing Society

PACIFICA FORUM
28-30 May 1991

Canadian Centre for
Studies in Publishing
Simon Fraser University
at Harbour Centre

515 W. Hastings St.
Vancouver, BC
Canada V6B 5K3
Tel: 604/291.5078
Fax: 604/291.5098

Canada Pacific
Publishing Society

Secretariat
1615 Venables St.
Vancouver, BC
Canada V5L 2H1

Canadian Centre for
Studies in Publishing
Simon Fraser University

Canada Pacific
Publishing Society

PACIFICA FORUM
28-30 May 1991

515 W. Hastings St.
Vancouver, BC
Canada V6B 5K3
Tel: 604/291.5078
Fax: 604/291.5098

Another successful use of the
wave form is this design created
for the Canadian Pacific Publishing Society of Vancouver, BC. It
was developed by designers
Raymond Mah and **Gek-Bee
Spangler** of RayMahDesign, Inc..
Here is a compelling use of color
and paper with the combination
of freeform, mechanical line art
and typography.

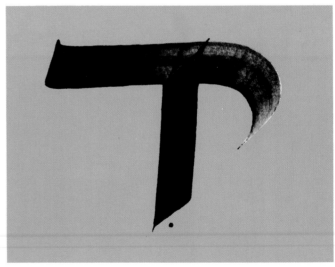

Here are two ID spots developed by **Gun Larson** of Sweden. *Top,* this piece was for The American Book Awards certificate which was presented together with a Louise Nevelson sculpture to the winning entries. The careful drawing of the letter forms has not denied the sense of freedom and flow in this hand created design. *Right,* a monogram style logo for Tore Persson, architect and building consultant. Here he used a wooden stick with Chinese ink.

Carl S. Mazer created these design spots for a series
of events and products for R. H. Macy & Co., Inc., of
New York. *Top left,* a spot for Parasport young
men's activewear. This symbol acts like a gesture
drawing to create the sense of youthful activity. *Top
right,* a more fashion-directed image for a women's
athleticwear shop. This image has the look of sports,
while not denying the fashion statements made by
the garments. The design in the middle was created
for a Valentine's Day promotion. This is a very
feminine and romantic free script. The final piece
was designed for a women's active footwear shop.
Its boldness has a sense of durablity and style.

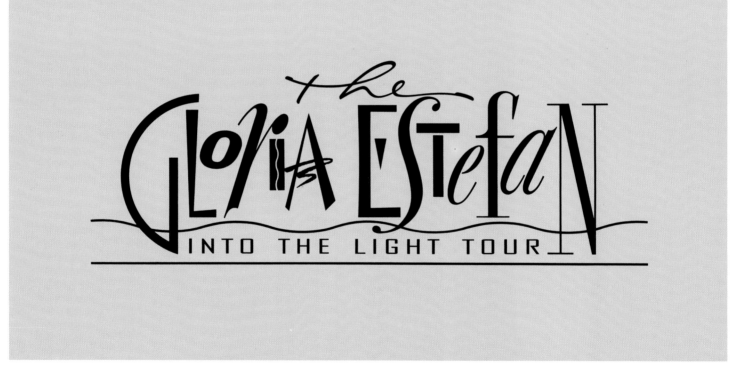

Tim Girvin has designed these two images for the entertainment world which has its own unique needs and demands: quick identification with product and easy access to the type of entertainment. The movie title *(top)* communicates the serious yet natural content of this production. And the title *(bottom)* gives this tour a festival attitude and the look of high-powered variety.

Art direction and
scenic design for
film, television, theatre
and advertising.

Interior design for
commercial and
residential spaces.

Exhibition design
for museums and
gala events.

Richard Carbotti
Winona Taylor
40 Cranston Ave.
Newport RI 02840
401 846 7794
Karen Anderson
NY 212 966 1213
Julie Hodgess
London 01 221 1964

Raphael Boguslav created this image for
the Carbotti/Taylor design firm in Newport,
Rhode Island. This is a wonderful combination of a beautifully handscripted logo
carefully placed on a colored paper
background.

On this page there are four images created by **Ron Brancato** of Rochester, NY, for four quite different clients. *(Left)*, "50. Hochzeitstag" was designed for Kodak International Exhibits. *(Top right)*, for the Rochester Institute of Technology's dance company. *(Center)*, a commemorative image for Good Shepherd Church. *(Bottom)*, a stylish look for a boutique. Each captures the moods and styles of a divergent clientele and shows the artist's ability to adapt his talent to the separate needs of each.

BRENDA WALTON
CALLIGRAPHY AND ILLUSTRATION
POST OFFICE BOX 161976
SACRAMENTO, CALIFORNIA 95816

BRENDA WALTON
CALLIGRAPHY AND ILLUSTRATION
POST OFFICE BOX 161976
SACRAMENTO, CALIFORNIA 95816
TELEPHONE: 916.456.5833

BRENDA WALTON
CALLIGRAPHY AND ILLUSTRATION
POST OFFICE BOX 161976
SACRAMENTO, CALIFORNIA 95816
TELEPHONE: 916.456.5833

Brenda Walton has created for her own
stationery this delicate imagery combining illustrations from nature, refined
typography and embossed hand lettering. This is an inviting design piece that
welcomes you into its midst.

This free-flowing image *(top)* was designed for Wilson/Muñoz & Associates, Inc., by **Joey Hannaford**. Since this is an architectural and interior design firm, this imagery is very appropriate.

Colleen has designed a delightful logo for this silk flower store *(right)*. Its simplicity and elegance fits the product well and establishes a quick connection with the consumer.

Colleen designed this logo *(top)* for the Handel & Haydn
Society with its appropriate modernized classical look. *Below,*
with Dorothy Cullinane of Hemlock Design, she created this
Express/fms logo which truly has the "express" look to it.

Top, a unique example of the use of the brush-stroke as a spontaneous gesture drawing done here to suggest the lowercase "d". This design was created by **Susan Skarsgard** for Dignitas and shows her special facility with the quick textured brush-stroke. *Below*, a more studied but still free-flowing script that displays a strong sense of design as well as artistry.

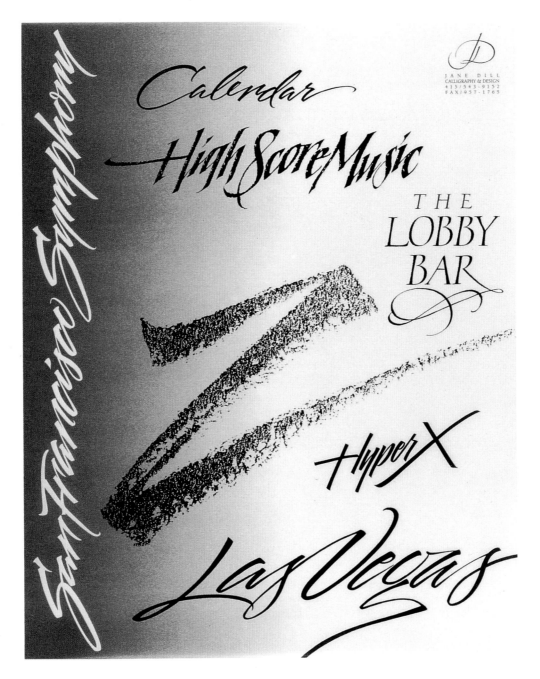

This is a self-promotion piece produced by **Jane Dill** to display her many freehand styles. She has a wonderful sense of flair and movement which this piece demonstrates. *Below,* more examples of her work with logos and titles.

440 EAST 62 ST. NEW YORK, NY 10021 PRINT (212) 752-6090 TV (212) 752-4450 FAX (212) 752-1071

440 E 62 ST. NY, NY 10021 (212) 752-4450 FAX (212) 752-1071

440 EAST 62 STREET

NEW YORK, NY 10021

PRINT (212) 752-6090

TV (212) 752-4450

FAX (212) 752-1071

Here designers **Mike Quon** and **Eileen Fogarty** of Mike Quon Design Office, Inc., have combined with Art Director Sandy Leigh to create this whimsical design image for the firm FunnyFace Models. Its lighthearted use of the brushstroke clearly projects the image of the company name and product.

Gallery

The following section completes our investigation into the world of modern freehand graphics. These pages display examples of fine art that enlist the free brushstroke and penstroke. Thus anyone who loves this kind of visual expression can see it in it's purest and most expressive form. This section is also offered to the viewer as an opportunity to discover new ideas that could be equally viable when adapted to applied commercial situations. No book about freehand graphics would be complete without showing some of the beauty and scope of the unrestricted free hand in fine art.

Barefoot Summer, Rose Folsom

Riot in Red Square, Rose Folsom

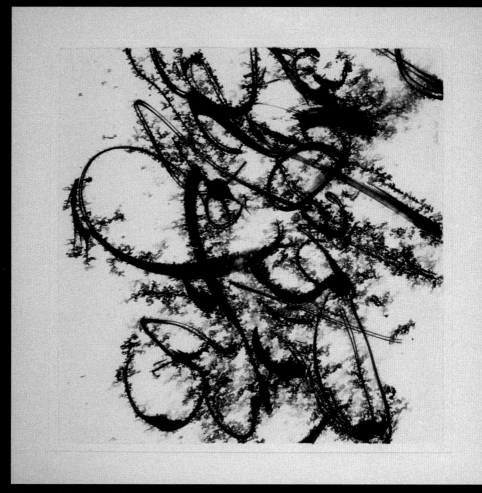

The Loved One, Rose Folsom

Spring, Rick Cusick

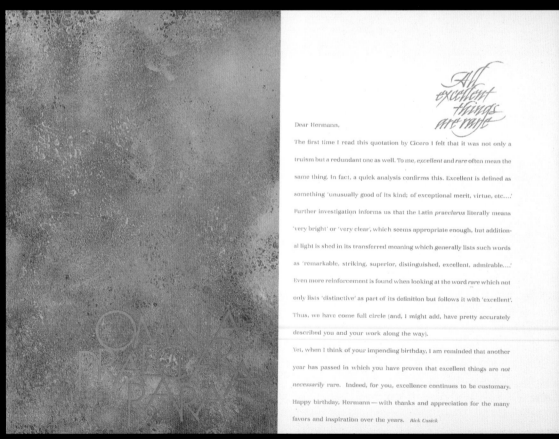

Paradox for HZ, birthday greetings to Hermann Zapf, Rick Cusick

Roundel of the Seasons, Sheila Waters

Heritage I, Howard Glasser

Heritage II, Howard Glasser

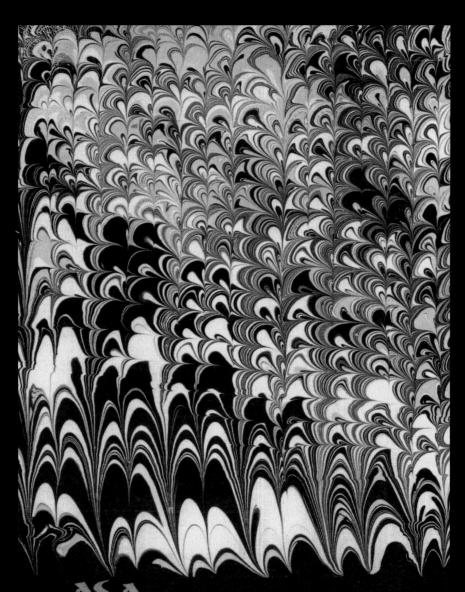

AS A
ROARING LION & A
so is a wicked ruler BEAR
28/15 over the poor people

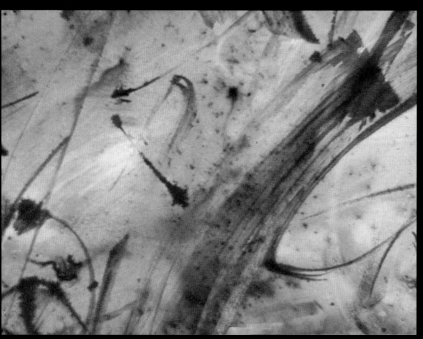

Reed II, Rose Folsom

Dance Around in Yer Bones, Rose Folsom

An exemplar for an almost totally illegible and useless script, Raphael Boguslav

On fine spring days the Capitals and the lower case played together

On fine spring days the Capitals and the lower case played together, Raphael Boguslav

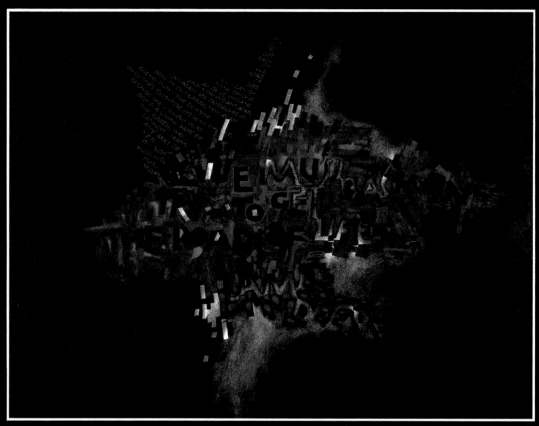

Lame Deer's words, Nancy Culmone

Friend, Nancy Culmone

Black Elk's words, Nancy Culmone

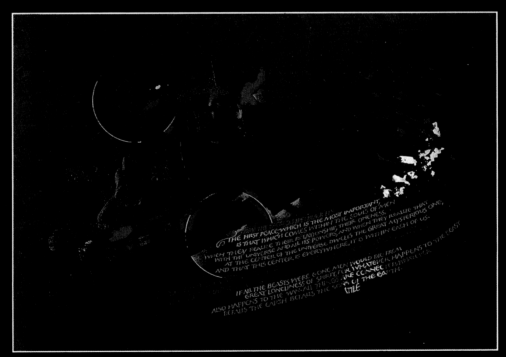

Reflections 1, Nancy Culmone

I want to be an
outrageous Old Woman
who never gets called 'old lady'
I want to get leaner and meaner
sharp-edged & earth-colored
'till I disincorp=
orate
from
sheer

Joy, Eliza Shulte

Alphabet, Eliza Shulte

Hua, Flower, Terry Louie

Variations on the Letter "A," Larry Brady

LITTERA SCRIPTA MANET

HORACE

Littera Scripta Manet, Larry Brady

All is a Gift, Larry Brady

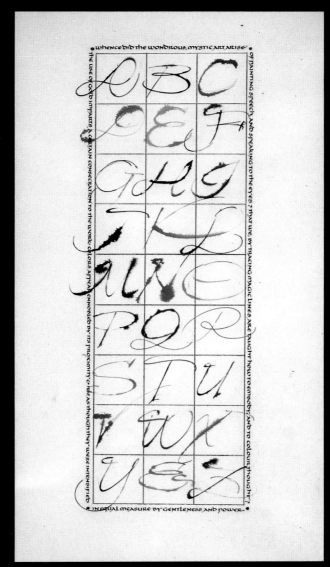

Whence Did the Wondrous, Mystic Art Arise, Marsha Brady

Alphabet, Marsha Brady

Index of Contributors

Shigeru Akizuki
815, 4-27-32 Ikejiri
Setagaya-Ku
Tokyo 154 Japan

Jack Anderson/Julia Lapine
Hornall Anderson Design Works
1008 Western Ave. 6th Floor
Seattle,WA 98104

Primo Angeli Inc.
590 Folsom St.
San Francisco, CA 94105

Peter Antipas
The Berni Co.
666 Steamboat Rd.
Greenwich, CT 06830

Felix Beltran
Felix Beltran & Asociados
Apartado Postal M-10733
Mexico 06000 DF Mexico

Paul Beluk/Mark Eckstein
The Berni Co.
666 Steamboat Rd.
Greenwich, CT 06830

Anthony Bloch
Anthony Bloch Calligraphy Design
854 W. 181 St.
New York, NY 10033

Raphael Boguslav
50 Old Beach Rd. A2
Newport, RI 02840

Robert Boyajian
511 Third Ave.
New York, NY 10016

Larry & Marsha Brady
Brady Design
11561 Harrisburg Rd.
Los Alamitos, CA 90720

Ron Brancato
333 N. Plymouth Ave. (2nd Floor)
Rochester, NY 14608

Paul M. Breeden
Box 40a, Route 200
Sullivan, ME 04689

Sherry Bringham
1804 Arlington Ave.
El Cerrito, CA 94530

Dia Calhoun
Design 26
116 West Denny Way
Seattle, WA 98119-4206

Thomas Carnase
Carnase Inc.
30 East 21 St.
New York, NY 10010

Kenneth Willis Cato
Cato Design Inc.
Pty Limited
254 Swan Street
Victoria 3121
Australia

Ivan Chermayeff
Chermayeff & Geismar Inc.
15 East 26th St.
New York, NY 10010

Rowennie Cheng
Bowen Designs
36 Tarlton Rd.
Toronto, Ontario 5MP 2M4

Colleen
25 Stanton Rd.
Brookline, MA 02146-6806

Bob Conge
28 Harper Street
Rochester, NY 14607

Nancy Culmone
P.O. Box 1425
Littleton, MA 01460

Jocelyn Curry
103 Northwest 200th
Seattle, WA 98177

Rick Cusick
7501 Westgate
Lenexa, KS 66216

Georgia Deaver
1045 Sansome St. Suite 311
San Franciso, CA 94111

Claude Dieterich A.
110 11th St., Apt. 303
Miami Beach, FL 33139

Jane Dill
123 Townsend St. 525
San Francisco, CA 94107

Fritz Eberhardt
852 Salford Station Rd.
Schwenksville, PA 19473

Richard Emery Design, Inc.
79 Eastern Ave.
Essex, MA 01929

Jean Evans
142 Garden St.
Cambridge, MA 02138

Rose Farber
Lewis & Gace
Fourth Floor
One Bridge Plaza
Fort Lee, NJ 07024

Hans Flink Design, Inc.
7-11 South Broadway
White Plains, NY 10601

Rose Folsom
908 Hudson Ave.
Takoma Park, MD 20912

Denise Foreman Graphic Design
4/20 Wylde Street
Bellevue Gardens Potts Point
Sydney, Australia NSW 2011

Steff Geissbuhler
Chermayeff & Geismar Inc.
15 East 26th St.
New York, NY 10010

Tim Girvin
Tim Girvin Design, Inc.
1601 2nd Ave. 5th Floor
Seattle, WA 98101-1575

Howard Glasser
28 Forge Rd.
Assonet, MA 02702

Joan Iverson Goswell
RDS Box 281
Sandy Hill Rd.
Valencia, PA 16059

Christopher Haanes
Hesselberggt 3
0555 Oslo, Norway

Joey Hannaford
Hannaford Designs
675 Drewry St. Studio 4
Atlanta, GA 30306

Barbara Harper
GE Graphic Communications
3135 Easton Turnpike
Fairfield, CT 06431

Kevin Horvath
17733 Farley St.
Overland Park, KS 66213

Jim Hillis/Roger Lundquist
Hillis Mackey & Co.
1550 Utica Ave. South No. 745
Minneapolis, MN 55416

Karlgeorg Hoefer
Weilburger Weg 7
6050 Offenbach am Main
Germany

Iskra Johnson
Iskra Lettering Design
1605 12th #26
Seattle, WA 98122

Hideyoki Kawarasaki
5-6-6-403 Tsurukawa
Machida City
Tokyo 194-01
Japan

Jennings Ku
The Hongkong and Shanghai Banking
    Corp. Ltd.
Level 18, 1 Queen's Rd., Central
Hong Kong

Gun Larson
Gun Larson Design Studio
Tygelsjovagen 62
S-230 42 Tygelsjo
Sweden

Richard Lipton
26 Mather St.
Dorchester, MA 02124

Terry Louie
3550 19th St.
San Francisco, CA 94110

Raymond Mah
RayMahDesign, Inc.
326 West Pender St.
Vancouver, BC V6B 1T1
Canada

Bernard Maisner/Jackie Meyer
Warner Books
666 5th Ave.
New York, NY 10103

Carl S. Mazer
R.H. Macy & Co., Inc.
151 W. 34th St.
New York, NY 10001

Karina Meister
Ten Kate Straat 65
1053 BZ Amsterdam
The Netherlands

Gayle Monkkonen
Scribble
1804 Belmont Rd. NW
Washington, D.C. 20009

Minoru Morita
Minoru Morita Graphic Design
192 Bible St.
Cos Cob, CT 06807

Chee Wang Ng.
130 Water Street 3H
New York, NY 10005-1622

Larry Ottino
The Ace Group
149 West 27th St.
New York, NY 10001

Ruth Pettis
689 Central Ave. #15
St. Petersburg, FL 33701

Mike Quon
Mike Quon Design Office
568 Broadway
New York, NY 10012

Frank Riccio
33 Eames Blvd.
Black Rock, CT 06605

Carl Rohrs
228 Ocean View
Santa Cruz, CA 95062

Ricardo Rousselot
Gran Via de Carlos III
97-J1°B 08028 Barcelona
Spain

Eliza Schulte Lettering Design
481 W. Judd St.
Woodstock, IL 60098

Paul Shaw
Paul Shaw Letter Design
785 West End Ave.
New York, NY 10025

Susan Skarsgard
1537 Natalie Lane, Suite #214
Ann Arbor, MI 48105

Bonnie Spiegel
121 William St.
Portland, ME 04103

Henry Steiner
Graphic Communications Ltd.
28c Conduit Rd.
Hong Kong

John Stevens
53 Clearmeadow Dr.
E. Meadow, N.Y. 11554

Fred Troller
Troller Associates
12 Harbor Lane
Rye, NY 10580

Edward Vartanian Design
114 Capuano Ave.
Crantson, RI 02920

Brenda Walton
Calligraphy & Illustration
14 Midway Ct.
Sacramento, CA 95817

Julian Waters
9509 Aspenwood Place
10153 Peanut Mill Dr.
Garthensburg, MD 20882

Sheila Waters
20740 Warfield Ct.
Gaithersburg, MD 20879

Patricia Weisberg
382 Central Park West
16V
New York, NY 10025

Jim Williams
Jim Williams Associates
130 West 42nd St.
New York, NY 10036